ABOUT THE AUTHOR

A writer of fund-raising letters is judged by his or her results.

Arthur L. Cone started his letter-writing career by helping a major publishing company, Prentice-Hall, sell books by mail. Then, he spent a decade with another major publishing company, where his direct-mail campaigns produced so many sales that the firm's bonus system was changed to prevent him from doubling his salary.

Mr. Cone's next move was into fund-raising. He went to the Washington, D.C. area to become copy chief for a prominent direct-mail fund-raising consulting firm, strong in political causes. From there, he went out on his own as a free lance writer. In 1971, he began freelance work for Epsilon Data Management, then a small computer-service group with 13 college fraternities as fund-raising clients. With marked assistance from Mr. Cone's writing, Epsilon grew from a nucleus of four founders into a corporation with more than 700 employees and offices from coast to coast.

Those are some of the results of Mr. Cone's career. But others —
even more convincing — will become apparent to you once you
begin to read this book. The majority of the fund-raising letters that
illustrate the author's points were originally written by Mr. Cone for
various nonprofit clients. What emerges is a glimpse of an author of
tremendous imagination and skill. The variety of client-causes bog-
gles the mind; he seems to have worked for everybody at one time
or another. And the approaches that Mr. Cone has devised to tap the
philanthropic potentials of this vast array of clients represent a bril-
liant exercise in ingenuity and ability.

In this book, Mr. Cone explains how to ''go and do likewise.'' It will be
a profitable lesson.

While specializing in fund-raising letters, Mr. Cone is also the author
of several other books, two of them expressions of his love and
knowledge of the outdoors: ''Fishing Made Easy'' and ''The Complete Guide to Hunting.'' With his wife, Joan, and a veterinarian
friend, he also authored ''Feeding Fido,'' a book on the proper feeding of dogs.

Mr. Cone has a B.A. degree from Wesleyan University and an
M.B.A. degree from New York University. He lives a writer's life in
Williamsburg, Va. within a short stroll of tennis courts, the swim-
ming pool, and his fishing boat.   *W.F.B.*

HOW TO CREATE AND USE

SOLID GOLD FUND-RAISING LETTERS

By Arthur Lambert Cone Jr.

FUND RAISING INSTITUTE
A Division of The Taft Group

To Joan—who makes everything seem like fun

Library of Congress Catalog Card Number: 87-81191
ISBN 0-930807-04-9

CONTENTS

Foreword

1. Know Your Prospects 1

   What Makes Them Tick?
   How to Test Their Reaction
   How to Find Them

2. What to Do Before You Write. 7

   Pin Down Your Theme
   Focus on Your Basic Purpose
   Make 'Negative' Appeals 'Positive'
   Plan How to Involve the Prospect
   Consider Personalizing the Letter

3. Ways to Master an 'Easy' Writing Style. 47

   Think Short
   Speak the Prospect's Language
   Brighten Your Vocabulary
   Use Punctuation for Meaning
   Make Grammar Work for You
   Use Criticism Creatively
   Know Yourself

4. Seven Steps to a Profitable Letter 67

   The Right Way to Begin
   How to Explain Why You're Writing
   How to Make It Believable
   How to Ask for the Money
   The Right Way to Close
   How to Pick the Signer
   Ways to Make Your P.S. Pay Off

5. Profitable Ways to Package Your Letter 97

   Mailing Envelopes That Increase Gifts
   How to Design a Gift Form
   Tips on Gift Envelopes
   Will Additional Inserts Raise More?

6. How to Raise Maximum Dollars 137

   Plan Your Mailing Program
   Raise the Donor's Giving Level
   Pick the Best Mailing Date and Frequency
   Save Money on Production

   A Final Word

FOREWORD

This book is different. There are plenty of books that show examples of letters to be used in fund-raising. But, very few — if any — of these become deeply involved in telling you how to write those letters effectively. Yet the competitive nature of fund-raising today, and the high costs of production and postage, make effective writing essential to success.

So in this book, you will learn how to gauge your fund-raising prospects and what to consider before writing to them. You'll learn how to come up with the ideas that let you develop an effective writing style.

Here are the ground rules I've followed. The focus of this book is on writing — writing letters. It's not a book on "direct-mail." So it will only touch lightly on the related elements involved in a mailing, such as envelopes, gift forms, tests, lists, inserts, and so forth. Every main point will be illustrated by examples taken from successful letters. We may discuss theory, but we'll also discover its practical applications — the profitable ones. Most importantly, we will try to be absolutely certain that your investment in this volume pays financial dividends this year, next year, and in all the years to come.

The rules are here, the guides are here, the examples are here, and most importantly the basics are here. While fads may come and go, the basics of successful fund-raising by mail remain suprisingly the same.

In writing this book, I have been helped by many good friends: Action on Smoking & Health; Epsilon Data Management, Inc.; Jean and Marty Martensen; Response Development Corporation; I. Brewster Terry; and Mrs. Alfreda Winnings. William F. Balthaser, editorial director of the Fund-Raising Institute, and his colleagues also deserve credit. The success of this book rests upon the wonderful cooperation of these and other friends, colleagues and critics, a few of whom include: Serap Akisoglu, David Austin, William Baker, Carol Bonnar, Larry Brown, H.J. Bryant, Ray P. Carter, Edward Coyle, John Daniels, Robert J. Desmond, Dawn F. Dreschler, Ann M. Felber, John M. Fisher, Winston Forrest, Alan Gottlieb,

Mary Hanewall, W.R. Hutchinson, Philip Kent, James Kerns, Kay Kirman, Steve Lawrence, Candy Lightner, Janet Michaels, Vickey Monrean, Frances Myers, Michael Nolan, Charles J. Orasin, Charles Orndorf, Lisa R. Peinhoff, Jacquelyn R. Pinchback, Al Rathert, Franklin Salisbury, Ronnie Schaer, Gary Schrenk, Suzanne Smith, Marcia Snyder, Cindy Joyce Speaker, Chester Tolson, Richard A. Viguerie, Amy Weickert, Father Tom Westhoven, Forrest Williamson, Grant Wills, and Robert Wobrock.

Also, American Fund for Dental Health; American Health Assistance Foundation; American Hiking Society; American Humane Association; American Security Council; Augusta Chronicle-Herald; The Ben Franklin Press; The Braille Institute; Camp Little Hawk; Chesapeake Bay Foundation; The Children's Hospital Foundation; Citizens Committee for the Right to Keep and Bear Arms; Colonial Williamsburg Fund; The Conservative Caucus Foundation; Craver, Mathews, Smith & Company; Foster Parents Plan; George Washington University; Good Shepherd Lutheran Home; Greenpeace; Handgun Control; Hour of Power; IndependentAction; International Lutheran Layman's League; Mothers Against Drunk Drivers; Morgan Memorial Inc.; National Foundation for Cancer Research; National RP Foundation; National Rifle Association; National Rifle Association/International Shooter Development Fund Inc.; Native American Rights Fund; The Nature Conservancy; Planned Parenthood Federation of America; Planned Parenthood of Southeasetern Virginia, Inc.; Russ Reid Co.; St. Joseph's School; US Ski Educational Foundation; The Viguerie Company; The Washington Hospital Center; World Wildlife Fund; and YMCA of Greater New York.

Arthur Lambert Cone Jr.

Some mail appeals raise enormous sums of money while others don't even repay their postage costs. There are many reasons for success and failure in the competitive world of fund-raising by mail. But perhaps the most significant single requirement for success is to know your market — to know to whom you're writing and what makes them tick.

You must understand the needs, desires, emotions, and goals of the persons to whom your mailing is directed. You must take the time to discover what they seek, and why they give. Only then do you have any business trying to write to them. Raising money is difficult enough, even with a sympathetic audience. You cannot force anyone to sit quietly, concentrate on your mailing, and absorb all the emotional and practical points you intend to make. So how are you going to entice someone you have never met into opening an envelope, agreeing with what you have to say, and actually responding with a check? The secret is in knowing your prospects. Here's how you do it.

1 FRI

WHAT MAKES THEM TICK?

Before you even begin to think about your message, your first task — call it market research if you wish — is to establish the criteria that define a suitable prospect. Then you'll know to whom you're writing. And you'll know what may motivate them to give. You'll be looking for three key things.

Donor status.   Because they gave recently, active donors are your best prospects. Obviously, they understand and approve of your goals. They have proven they are willing to underwrite your organization with their contributions. So study your current donors; find what they have in common that makes them donors. Others who also have been asked didn't give. What is there about them that sets them apart from the common herd of humanity? Next, study your former active donors. Try to pin down how former donors differ from active donors. Have they moved away, died or retired? Did they lose interest in your cause, and, if so, why?

1

Demographics. Consider gender. Are your best prospects male, or female, or a mixture of both? What about age? Are they young, middle-aged, or elderly? Are they well-to-do or people of average means? (But, remember, sometimes the best givers are not the most wealthy.) Do they share any religious or ethnic characteristics in common? Where do your best prospects live: on farms, in small towns, in middle-size or large cities? Are they concentrated in certain states and regions such as the South or Middle West? There may be a reason why they are, and you must understand it.

Motivation. Answer the question, "Why do people support us?" Perhaps your prospects have blind, or mentally handicapped children. Possibly they believe Judgement Day is approaching. They may have ties to a certain university or own a pet. The point is that, as a group, most of your best prospects will have one or more emotional ties in common. You must sort these out, and then consider where to turn to find other people who are similar in their tastes, feelings, convictions, psychic needs, and outlooks.

HOW TO TEST THEIR REACTION

There are lots of different ways of saying or asking the same thing. Which is the best way?

Your knowledge of your prospects will help you make a rough sorting of your letter-writing options. Yet the best way to prove the answer (and there *is* a "best" way) is to test. Don't believe your opinions until they're proven. Test one letter against another; test one paragraph against another; test one idea against another. You can even test one complete mailing package against another.

And when you test, remember one firm rule: Test only one variable at a time. Don't test paragraph "A" on one list and paragraph "B" on a totally different list. That equals two variables: the paragraphs and the lists. Rather, test your two paragraphs on equal and similar samples taken from the same list. Then there's only one variable: the paragraph.

Study your test results carefully; follow them for a while. Evaluate them qualitatively as well as quantitatively. Certain types of appeals — particularly those involving premiums, sweepstakes, and other gimmicks — may produce apparently good results, at least in the number of contributions received. However, you may find that these donors make only minimum contributions, and very few of their gifts can be repeated next year or upgraded. If this is the case, the mailing may turn out to be a poor investment. So follow the performance of donors obtained through the test for a while. Don't react strongly to the initial response. Hold your budget back until the donors have established a track record. Consider their repeat giving and upgrading to be part of the test. Make sure the odds are clearly in your favor before you make the big investment.

HOW TO FIND THEM

Assume you now know your best prospects, what makes them tick, and what appeals they respond to most generously. Then your next job is to find many more people just like them. In direct-mail fundraising, that means you must discover new prospect lists. Without delving too deeply into the direct-mail field, here are some basic tips on how to find and use such lists.

- Small lists are more productive than larger lists. (The best explanation for this is that they are not watered down by marginal prospects.)

- Lists compiled from directories or similar sources will not produce as well as those that contain names of individuals who replied to direct-mail fund-raising appeals or some other form of direct-response advertising. (The obvious reason is that any compiled list includes many persons who are simply not responsive to such advertising.)

- As we have touched on earlier, the closer you can come to people who are similar or identical to your present donors, the better a list will be. (People with similar tastes, likes, habits and habitations will generally follow a similar giving pattern.)

- You can obtain new prospect lists by compiling them yourself, by renting them from others, or by exchanging use of your list for that of a similar cause.

Let's look for a moment at this third option: exchanging. The best way to arrange a list exchange is to decide which organizations might have lists that could work well for you. Consider groups in your general field. Phone or write, and ask if they are interested in a name swap with you. Some will respond with an outright "no." Generally, there is little you can do to change such a response.

But with organizations that say "yes" or "maybe," you will probably hold a meeting, or exchange correspondence, with the aim of establishing a contractual relationship. Such a relationship is often overseen by a professional list broker who is paid a fee to run the exchange.

The first thing each party should do with a list obtained in an exchange is test it with a mailing package that's known to pull a good response — called a "control" package in the direct-mail field. Should these tests be satisfactory to both parties, they can easily be expanded. If either party is unhappy, that will probably end the exchange.

• Proper testing of lists is an exercise in statistics. Most list owners require that you take a minimum test quantity, usually 5,000 names. With a list of 50,000 or so, this is a fair enough test. With a very large list, you may want to do a series of tests — each one larger than the last.

One point to recognize is that you cannot test without a "control" — a mailing package that you have used enough to know its approximate results when sent to a good list. Compare the control's performance when sent to the new list against the control's past performance when used with proven lists. Keep all the variables (such as time of year) constant except for that of the list.

List testing is an expensive but necessary evil. You *must* test if you want to discover new lists that will add responsive names to your donor file. If you don't add names, that file will wither away. Testing involves complex statistical records and expensive, short printing runs. It's difficult to break even or make a profit on a test mailing, so you should consider it as an investment.

To maximize the return on that investment, only test those lists that appear to have a good chance for success. The closer the persons on the list come to your own donors' profile — in interests, income, geographic location, and so forth — the better you will do. Naturally, you will prefer lists made up of individuals who are "mail responsive" — that is, who have been placed upon the list because they replied to a direct-mail appeal, hopefully one similar to yours.

- Some appeals are so limited they simply cannot utilize direct-mail, at least not extensively. For example, many colleges cannot go far beyond their alumni. Or another example: The general public is either frightened, unsympathetic, or both, about mental health problems. For causes in that field, sometimes the only reliable sources of new names are lists of contributors to various other mental health causes — or if you can find them, lists of people with a personal or family relationship to mental retardation, insanity, and other mental problems.

Many first-rate fund-raising executives have been totally frustrated by an inability to raise money by mail for causes that the broad, general public simply refuses to support.

In summary.　This does not pretend to be a book on direct-mail. It focuses on a single, crucial area of direct-mail — how to write a really effective fund-raising letter. But your letter will not work unless you apply many other basic market-research and direct-mail techniques. This chapter has been designed to raise your awareness of these techniques and to help you understand how they affect the results of your letter. Hopefully, your interest will be whetted, and you will eventually go on to learn more about the impact of these direct-mail techniques on your letter's results.

PIN DOWN YOUR THEME

The first chapter of this book discussed the need to understand your market, who your prospects are, where they live, and everything else about them that is pertinent. Now we must contemplate what proposition we put before them. And then we must decide on the most effective technique for selling that proposition in a fund-raising package. There are only a few variations. The following are the basic themes for nearly every fund-raising package that may concern you.

Building and equipment purchases.   You don't need to create an emergency to indicate a genuine need for new or renovated facilities or equipment. The Albert Einstein Medical Center, the San Diego Zoological Society, Haverford College, and institutions everywhere successfully ask for funds for physical expansion or new equipment. Often, the focus is on the exciting new programs the new building or equipment will make possible. You can base your appeal on those kinds of goals. You can build all sorts of things, but here's an appeal that combines a building program and a deadline — a kind of emergency.

```
Dear Mr. Sample:

     This is a difficult letter for me to write you.  But
I know you've helped out before so I think you'll want to
read every word.  It's important.

     Unless we break ground for our Vietnam Veterans Mem-
orial on March 1st, we cannot dedicate it on Veterans Day,
November 11, 19   as we've planned.

     But we are still thousands of dollars short.

     So, I must ask you for extra help...a major commit-
ment on your part.  It isn't easy for me.  But I must
because there is no choice.

     I'm asking you for a very special gift -- a
contribution of $50 -- a gift larger than you've ever given
before.
```

Emergency funds. Individuals have emergencies in their lives. So do nonprofit groups. "Our building must be repaired this year or it will be condemned." "Innocent children will die of starvation within a month unless we can raise money to help them." "We must raise matching funds within the next four weeks, or lose $100,000." An emergency may be any urgent situation that suddenly confronts an organization or an individual. But how many emergencies can a cause have?

In Aesop's fable, the boy who cried "Wolf!" once too often was devoured by a real wolf when everyone ignored his suddenly-legitimate cries for help. But in real life, several religious, political, and other groups call for emergency assistance at least a dozen times annually. And apparently they obtain it. Why do emergency appeals work so well? Let's look at some. These letter openings come from a group of varied emergency appeals. They have one thing in common. They don't hesitate to give the supporting facts.

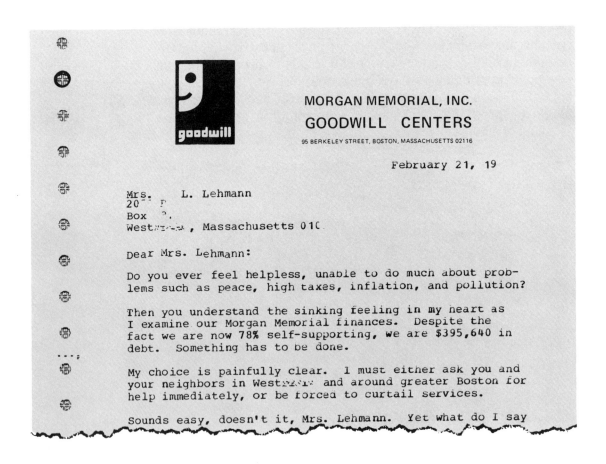

MORGAN MEMORIAL, INC.

GOODWILL CENTERS

95 BERKELEY STREET, BOSTON, MASSACHUSETTS 02116

February 21, 19

Mrs. L. Lehmann
20 ̄ ̄ ꞁ
Box ꞏ.
West⸱⸱⸱⸱⸱⸱, Massachusetts 01C

Dear Mrs. Lehmann:

Do you ever feel helpless, unable to do much about problems such as peace, high taxes, inflation, and pollution?

Then you understand the sinking feeling in my heart as
I examine our Morgan Memorial finances. Despite the
fact we are now 78% self-supporting, we are $395,640 in
debt. Something has to be done.

My choice is painfully clear. I must either ask you and
your neighbors in West⸱⸱⸱⸱⸱ and around greater Boston for
help immediately, or be forced to curtail services.

Sounds easy, doesn't it, Mrs. Lehmann. Yet what do I say

NRA
Political Victory Fund

Institute for Legislative Action
P.O. Box 7396, Washington, D.C. 20044

August 25, 19

Dear NRA Member:

We face an emergency and I need your help immediately.

Never before have we faced such nationwide attacks on our Constitutional right to keep and bear arms under the guise of "controlling crime."

Never before have we faced such serious challenges to firearms freedom by the candidates slated to run in several key states — like California, New York, Massachusetts, Minnesota, Ohio, and others — who, if elected, would impose their gun-ban credo on 50 percent of the nation's population, on millions of peaceful citizens like yourself who choose to own a handgun.

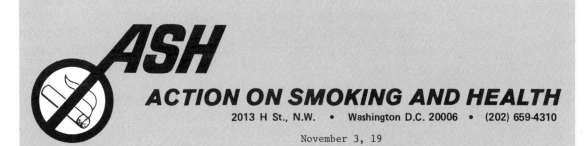

ASH

ACTION ON SMOKING AND HEALTH

2013 H St., N.W. • Washington D.C. 20006 • (202) 659-4310

November 3, 19

Mr. Arthur L. Cone, Jr.
P.O. Box ˉ9
Williamsburg, Virginia 231ᴜ.

Dear Art:

More than $30,000 in unpaid bills are on my desk as I write you today.

That's why ASH needs your immediate support in order to survive.

For while legal action is the most effective weapon against the tobacco industry efforts to sicken you and seduce your children, it can be costly.

9

```
                    America is in trouble, and
                we need your help before August 21st.


Dear Member,

    I'm writing this emergency letter because I think you under-
stand better than most the work we must do immediately to protect
America's wildlife and environment.

    Here's the hazardous situation we face as you read this...

        Right now, in Washington, the financial under-
        pinnings from many federal programs that help
        insure clean water, clean air, and which
        maintain and protect the environment have been
        cut.  These laws and regulations guard our
        country's natural beauty and health.  They are
```

Assistance to needy individuals.   Case histories bring a human dimension to fund-raising. The appeal of an abandoned or hungry child or a threatened baby is obvious. The plight of an elderly widow facing eviction was used effectively in an appeal letter from The Legal Aid Society of New York City. The need for funds to provide Indian children a school on their reservation brought contributions to The Native American Rights Fund.

If you have a good story, use it. (But unless you have written consent to do so, never refer to an actual person's name. You could get into legal trouble. A true story using pseudonyms instead of actual names is generally the least risky.) Everyone is interested in a good human interest story. If a case history is practical and available, it should be considered and used if possible. Here is a case history — one without the identification of any specific child — used by the YMCA.

YMCA
of Greater New York

422 Ninth Avenue, New York. N.Y. 10001   (212) 564-1300

Tommy is one of thousands of reasons why ...

you should support your "Y" today!

    He may live down the block, around the corner,
or in the apartment house next door.

    And when summer comes, and school is out, Tommy
and his lively young friends, both boys and girls, need
their neighborhood "Y". That's why I'm writing to ask
for your support.

    Youngsters come here to learn to swim, shoot baskets,
work on arts and crafts projects, attend day camp, and board
chartered buses for special trips.

    It's all especially important these days. For New
York City's school playgrounds now are padlocked all summer
to save money! With nowhere to go except dangerous parks,
and even more dangerous streets, neighborhood children need
the "Y" more than ever. It's a place where a city youngst

*This letter was written during a time when New York City was going
through a difficult economic period.*

And from the Braille Institute, a more generalized appeal on behalf of needy individuals.

BRAILLE INSTITUTE

Did you ever stop

to consider why

you almost never

see a blind child?

There are many of them...far more than you would suppose. But you won't see them riding bikes, surfing, or playing tennis. So it's easy to forget they are there.

Blindness at any age is tragic, but it seems even more so if you are seven years old. You may have no friends because you can't play outside with sighted children.

Blind children have very special needs. They must learn to move about and become at home with a big frightening world they cannot see. These boys and girls cannot see a flower, an ocean wave, or even Mommy or Daddy's face.

But we can't allow them to remain locked away in their dark prison. They need a special kind of help and caring to help set them free.

That's why I'm writing and asking you to do what you can for Braille Institute's Youth Program.

Medical research and disease control. Without good health, human life is hardly worth living. All of us seek to achieve and preserve it. Therefore, a letter aimed at funding medical research or disease control attracts many who hope their own lives and longevity may be benefitted. A medical research appeal works best when aimed at an audience that understands the problem from personal experience. For example, look at the P.S. of this appeal.

Dear Friend:

Even though we have never met, I've decided to write and ask you for help. After all, your life could depend on the pioneering work of your National Cytology Research Center.

We hope to make all death from cancer obsolete. Already we understand how to detect and cure six common types of cancer before fatal tumors appear. We've shown doctors how to find certain cancers in women up to nine years before these become active. As a result, nearly 100% are permanently cured.

Today we can find pre-cancer cells before malignant lung tumors develop, and actually stop lung cancer before it starts.

Your National Cytology Research Center is also responsible for methods which detect cervix or uterine cancer, early skin

Let me hear from you right away. I am looking forward to your early reply.

Sincerely yours,

H. Balthasar Lawrence, M.D.
President and Medical Director

P.S. Would you consider making a special gift in the name of a relative or close friend who has died of cancer? We must make faster progress. Cancer can be prevented and cured if we have enough money to discover how.

Animal welfare. Most of us love animals. Humane societies, animal shelters, and similar groups have a strong fund-raising appeal.

There is a crisis on your street ...
... and it's a crime! It exists even
though you may not be aware!

Look carefully, next time you go outdoors. You may see a hungry cat slinking behind a wall...or a dog eating garbage. These animals, abandoned or lost in your neighborhood, often spread disease or bite a child...that's one reason the C.J.S. Animal Shelter is so concerned about these homeless animals.

We nurse many of these waifs back to health, find them homes, give them the opportunity of knowing and returning love and affection.

When you join us as a member of the C.J.S. Animal Shelter, you help us reduce animal borne disease and the nation's number two reported health problem--dog bites. Additionally, you gain positive and highly worthwile benefits.

For example, if you own a pet, we will provide you with a special computer-recorded identification tag to help insure your pets safe return if lost.

Conservation.   Conservation causes attract those who want to make this world a better place by protecting air, water, wilderness, and animal life. These resources are endangered by the industrial revolution and its high, non-farm employment, by urban development and by exploitation of natural resources. Generally, a conservation appeal asks for help to stop the deterioration of our planet by so-called progress, to assist endangered species of plants and animals, or to restore our world to the pristine condition it once knew. Even organizations whose connection with the outdoors is only tenuous use conservation as a theme. (For example, a more efficient heating system will use less oil and reduce air pollution.) But here are two more genuine plugs for nature.

The Nature Conservancy

1800 North Kent Street, Arlington, Virginia 22209
(703) 524-3151

Dear Friend:

Do you remember when you were a child?

What has happened to the nearby fields and woods where you went to play, or the unpolluted lake or stream where you learned to swim?

Today, the open spaces you enjoyed near home are probably paved over or built upon. If your family had a vacation cottage at the shore or in the mountains, it's now surrounded by subdivisions.

Times have changed, haven't they? This is why I'm writing and inviting you to join The Nature Conservancy. We don't shout or wave signs. Instead, we quietly buy the remaining irreplaceable land threatened by commercial development. By quick action, we have saved many areas from the land speculators.

WORLD WILDLIFE FUND-U.S.

1601 CONNECTICUT AVENUE NW
WASHINGTON DC 20009

TELEPHONE: (202) 387–0800

RUSSELL E. TRAIN
PRESIDENT

You hear talk about the need

to save our planet's endangered wildlife...

...too often it's just talk.

        That's why I am writing to you today. For I assume that
you not only want to talk about it but that you are concerned
with what's been happening and want to do something about it.

        You know that many forms of life, once abundant, are now
vanishing forever.

        What can you do about it?

        You can accept this invitation to support World Wildlife
Fund.

        Since 1961, World Wildlife Fund has helped to rescue a
great number of mammals and birds from the brink of extinction.
It has created or supported 260 National Parks on five continents -
a total area almost twice the size of Texas - to provide wild

Politics/religion/legislation/special causes. The closing years of this 20th century may someday be remembered as "The Age of Obsessions." We live in an atmosphere that generates too much heat and too little basic logic. Many of us tend to look on issues in terms of "absolutes" instead of interpreting them in varying shades of gray. Some of us firmly believe our country will perish unless we enhance our national defense. Others preach that we all will be obliterated by nuclear disaster if we build more bombs. There are those who speak for and against handguns, abortion, capital punishment, and so forth.

But there is a bright side to everything. The same obsessive, single-issue constituencies that are the bane of government are a *boon* to fund-raisers. If you can develop a list of prospects who believe that the sky will fall if your ideas don't prevail, by all means tell them when it seems that the firmament is about to descend unless they act fast! They will support you generously. Here's a typical example.

Dear Potential Handgun Victim,

Only hours after Ronald Reagan was shot CBS news correspondent Bruce Morton reported that the attempt on the President's life would not affect handgun control legislation in the Congress. What kind of insanity is this? How could this be?

The answer is all too simple. It's because of the National Rifle Association and the powerful hold it has on Congress. The NRA year after year prevents Congress from passing handgun control legislation.

In fact, on the day President Reagan was wounded by a Saturday Night Special the NRA had planned to launch its attack on the 1968 law barring the importation of Saturday Night Specials. They only paused long enough for the headlines to fade on this handgun attack. The NRA is now hard at work to pass a bill known as the McCl...

Immortality: the 'Cult of Self.'   The more of us there are on this overcrowded chunk of matter we call Earth, the greater is our urge to stand out from the crowd as individuals. Also, knowing we must surely die, we have an intense desire to be remembered and thereby in a sense, to become immortal.

The desire to be admired, respected and remembered is one reason that, for more than a century, people have enjoyed — and paid for — the privilege of seeing their names printed in a concert or opera program. Carrying this theme further, mailings have achieved success by promising to carve a donor's name in marble, cast it in everlasting bronze, display it upon a certificate or plaque, or list it in perpetuity among institutional benefactors. The "Cult of Self" may be a crime in Soviet Russia. Yet it is something you, as a writer, are bound to respect and consider. The following opening sentences say it all!

<u>What will they say of you in days to come?</u>

Will they say you were a person of courage...one who was willing to give of himself to help those who were less fortunate?

Or will they point out that you showed little Christian charity towards fellow human beings who, for reasons over which they had no control, suffered the terrible affliction of mental illness?

In our competitive society, many are crying out for help with emotional and mental problems. The Meridian Homes's only reason for existence is to help them through consultation, education, and psycho-therapy within a framework of Christian love and concern.

Holidays and seasons. Christmas, Ramadan, Thanksgiving, New Year's Day, Hanukkah . . . holidays can often add a special cachet to a fund-raising appeal. They have emotional value. Because they are associated with joy, they make sadness and tragedy even more compelling.

Each season has special fund-raising themes of its own. Autumn has its falling leaves, football games, and bonfires. Spring has grass turning green, buds bursting into bloom — the reality of life being annually renewed. The bleak cold of winter helps justify an emergency, as does summer with asphalt melting and heat stifling the children, who are forced to play on deadly city streets.

This letter contrasts Thanksgiving with blindness.

NATIONAL GLAUCOMA RESEARCH PROGRAM

A PROGRAM OF THE AMERICAN HEALTH ASSISTANCE FOUNDATION

1700 K STREET. N.W., SUITE 405
WASHINGTON, D.C. 20006
(202) 466-4104

Eugene H. Michaels
President

Being Blind Does Hurt . . .

Especially at Thanksgiving

    That's why I am writing to ask you for this special personal favor.

    Before you sit down to your Thanksgiving Dinner on Thursday, November 26th, please take a moment to give thanks for your own ability to see and enjoy this wonderful world.

    For then I know you will resolve to continue helping the National Glaucoma Research Program win its continuing battle against one of America's leading causes of blindness.

    As you already realize, we need money to fund research at prestigious medical schools across the country. We want to

FOCUS ON YOUR BASIC PURPOSE

There are lots of ways to present an appeal and to make it interesting. You can use case histories, premiums, sweepstakes, and other techniques. But you must remember one vital element: your basic purpose for raising funds. Don't get so involved with "techniques" that you miss the main point of your letter. That main point should have top billing.

Here's how you do the job. First, you make sure that you, yourself, know exactly why the gift is being asked for. Nonprofit causes tend to need simply "money." You ask "why," and they'll tell you, "to pay the bills." But you've got to go a step or so beyond this pragmatic reasoning, asking, "What will be accomplished if this money is received?" and "Why will the prospective donor see this as a benefit?" If you can't get answers to these questions, stop.

You have nothing to write about.

People do not give significantly to sweepstakes or case histories, no matter how interesting they are. They give to support activities that they see as being beneficial to themselves or, at least, to how they think their world should be.

So uncover your basic purpose, define it clearly, and make sure it shines brightly (and early on) in your text. Here are two fine examples. You may not agree with the basic purposes of these fundraisers, but you do have to agree that the basic purposes aren't hidden. One letter makes it clear that you're in danger of losing your political clout for the remainder of the century. The other offers to protect you from unfair overseas competitors.

Your basic purpose must be the reason behind virtually every word and thought in your letter: Every anecdote, story, case history, and membership offer must tie in directly with the basic objectives of your cause. It must be clearly and well stated, as it is here.

MADE IN USA

Is Your Key

To Effective Action

Against Imports !

As a small manufacturer, you face unfair competition from
low- priced imports.

Based on cheap foreign labor and imitative technology, these
products hurt all Americans.

They make it harder to market your products, slash
individual and corporate buying power, and put fellow
citizens out of work.

The Ben Franklin Society is fighting back on your behalf.

MADE IN USA is our all-out project aimed to help small
businesses. You are invited to join this project now.
And because the Ben Franklin Society is non-profit (501 C-3),
your small voluntary dues are tax deductible.

As a Supporting Member, you have full use of MADE IN USA
and benefit by all our promotion and public relations.

TASK FORCE

May 24, 19

Mrs. J. Cone
P. O. Box 2
Williamsburg, Virginia 2318

Dear Mrs. Cone:

I'm writing today to ask for your help.

For you and I must take quick action to ensure that everything the Reagan Administration stands for is not defeated in the ' elections.

Specifically, President Reagan is in danger of losing his Republican Majority in the U.S. Senate for the rest of this century.

And I want to tell you as plainly as I can, what this means --- Ronald Reagan cannot continue reshaping our nation's future without the support and leadership of our Republican Senate Majority.

MAKE 'NEGATIVE' APPEALS 'POSITIVE'

In fund-raising, a "plus" generally beats a "minus."

This is true even though much successful fund-raising involves considerable "viewing with alarm." You may object to acid rain, child abuse or other negatives. If so, come up with a positive answer to the problem. While donors may be willing to make sacrifices for a cause, they do not want their precious gift wasted on a lost cause. Even in politics, where more people may vote against a candidate than for the opponent, they believe they are doing so in the cause of "good government" — the positive factor.

So involve the prospect in a positive way — building, assisting, creating, freeing, and improving — instead of opposing.

What could be more negative than having your child killed by a drunk driver? This letter is a perfect example of turning a "negative" into a "positive" by showing people how taking action will help eliminate the negative. People give to "save children" rather than to "stop drinking."

MADD

MOTHERS AGAINST DRUNK DRIVERS

**DRUNK DRIVERS KILL.
THEY SERIOUSLY INJURE.
AND THEY GET AWAY WITH IT!**

You ask, "What can I do about it?" Let me tell you what I'm doing and how you can help.

Candy Lightner

Dear Friend,

    I'm writing you today not just to tell you what happened to me, but to tell you what continues to happen to thousands of other innocent victims.

    But let me start at the beginning.

    On a beautiful spring afternoon in 1980, I drove home after a shopping trip and found my father and ex-husband waiting for me, their faces ashen and tears in their eyes.

    Steve, my ex-husband, said, "We've lost Cari."

    I patted him on the back and replied, "It's okay, we'll find her."

    "You don't understand," he said. "A man came along with a car, and killed her -- and left her to die."

    I couldn't believe him!

    So I quit my real estate job and founded an organization called MADD -- Mothers Against Drunk Drivers.

    It wasn't long before I began to get phone calls and letters from people who, like me, had had their loved ones killed by drunk drivers:

    . . . people like Cindi Lamb, the Maryland mother whose infant daughter was paralyzed for life from the shoulders down -- by a man whose traffic record had 56 separate entries, including three arrests for drunk driving.

In response to an avalanche of television, newspaper and magazine exposure, MADD has been able to expand nation- wide in less than two years.

Some people are amazed at what we've already done. We have established a victim assistance program to help the vic- tims affected by drunk driving accidents. We have supported legislation introduced on the federal level. We were respon- sible for a governor-appointed task force in California to solve the problem of drunk driving.

And our support was instrumental in legislation being passed which gives California the toughest anti-drunk-driving laws in the United States. In fact <u>the month after these laws</u> <u>went into effect, drunk driving arrests and deaths fell more</u> <u>than 20 percent!</u>

<u>I'm asking for your help to deal with this national crime</u> that kills and injures so many innocent victims every year. Will you stand with us?

We urgently need your gift of $20, $100, $25, $50 or whatever you can send. I need to hear you say you're behind us -- that you're willing to do what you can to help change the laws of this country.

Drunk drivers kill. They maim. They seriously injure. <u>And they get away with it</u>. Please help us fight back!

Yours very sincerely,

Candy Lightner

Candy Lightner

PLAN HOW TO INVOLVE THE PROSPECT

Part of a writer's job is to make a worthy cause become fascinating. That is the raison d'etre behind the varied "involvement" techniques that have developed in the direct-mail field. Involvement techniques such as those we'll describe in a moment help a cause stand out, attract attention, and seize the prospect's interest. They increase both the number of contributors and the average size of the contributions. All of these techniques have been used successfully — some by colleges and universities, others by hospitals, political parties, religious groups, and a broad range of issue-related appeals.

Guidelines. Before the examples, let's ask a basic question: Exactly what is an "involvement technique"? Here's a short essay on the subject.

Obviously, the major job — the most challenging job — of an appeal letter is to get the prospective donor to decide to make a gift and then to send it. But you've got to build to this climax in a series of easy, small steps. First, you must get the prospect interested in reading your appeal. One way to do this is to give him or her "something else" to do first, before you ask for money. So, many involvement techniques do just that; they ask the prospect to do something that doesn't represent as difficult a decision as the one about contributing money. The idea is that, once you persuade prospects to do something that doesn't necessarily involve a gift for your cause: 1) they will have been dissuaded from throwing your appeal into the trash, and 2) it will be easier to convince them to keep going and mail in a donation.

For example, instead of immediately asking for a gift, you ask the prospects for information about themselves or for their opinion. Then, after they have already decided to help you by providing information, you ask them to help further by sending money. It's a two-step process: first you involve them in helping, then you involve them in helping *with money*. If you do it right, the second decision (the one about the money) becomes easier for the prospect. So the number of gifts and the size of the average gift are apt to increase. (You're also apt to secure information you can put to good use.)

There are other ways to involve a prospect. You can ask someone to help by sending a post card to their senator urging action that will aid your cause. Or you can invite them to participate in a sweepstakes contest, or to join a membership group, or to paste your sticker on their automobile's bumper. But this brings up another question: How do you go about picking the right involvement technique? Here are guidelines to help you.

- Your ultimate consideration is the "bottom line," the net gift income that results from the appeal. Most (but not all) involvement devices mean added cost. First you want that added cost to pay for itself, and then you want it to produce still additional gift income.

- The involvement technique you pick must be appropriate to your cause and your appeal message. An art museum, for example, might find it sensible to run a sweepstakes contest where the prizes were paintings or trips to visit museums. But a sweepstakes of any kind might be wrong for a fundamentalist, Protestant religious group. Even if you use a questionnaire as an involvement technique, the questions should be closely related to your cause.

- Some involvement techniques — ones that are perfectly valid and appropriate — may frighten your group's decision-makers. So you should pick one with which your leadership is comfortable.

- As with most other direct-mail techniques, you should always test any involvement technique against a control mailing or against an identical mailing without the involvement device.

- You should recognize that there are some causes the public would rather not even hear about, and for them an involvement device may be absolutely necessary to obtain any response at all.

- Keep in mind that your objective is to produce maximum response and gift income at minimum cost. In addition, you intend to acquire new donors whose giving can be renewed and upgraded over the coming years. Some involvement devices will do this for you, and others will fail. Common sense may help you tell which is which, but back up common sense with cautious testing.

Now, here are a few sample involvement techniques.

Surveys.   The success of surveys as an involvement technique is based on a desire most of us have to influence events — to make our voice count, our opinion matter. Surveys are well suited to political or special interest causes, yet they can be adapted to nearly any fund-raising purpose. One guideline to follow is to assure your prospect that the results of a poll or survey will be presented to Congress, the Supreme Court, the American Bar Association, or whatever group you seek to influence. This will show your prospect that a response really does matter.

AMERICAN SECURITY COUNCIL
1101 17th Street, N.W., Washington, D.C. 20036

John M. Fisher
President

November 17, 19

Arthur L. Cone, Jr.
9_ ` ac Rd
Vienna, Virginia 22′

Dear Fellow American:

   Because you are an opinion leader in Vienna, you have been nominated to serve on our National Advisory Board and to participate in our 19   National Security Issues Poll.

   This is, of course, subject to your acceptance.

   To insure accurate poll tabulation, I have assigned an identification code to each prospective Board member. Your code number, Fellow American, is 2936.

   We want to release the results of this Poll to the President, the Congress and the press as early in ' as possible, so please return your vote today.

   Your vote is particularly important now because official Washington is <u>NOT</u> representing you and me in their decisions concerning our nation's survival!

SURVEY ON STRESS AND CANCER

SURVEY NUMBER: 1075953

Assigned to: 107 595 373 3   5 5

Mr. Damon P ⊃⁚
Box "
Williamsburg, VA   231⁚

Instructions: Answer questions below by checking appropriate box.
Important: Even if you don't complete it, it is critical to our results that you return it to us.

Note: Your answers will be tabulated with others. Your name will be held confidential in the tabulation.

Question 1:	Were you aware experts report as much as 70% of illness, including cancer, may be caused by stress? ☐ Yes ☐ No
Question 2:	Have you experienced any of the following situations within the last three (3) years? (Check all which apply to you) ☐ Death of your spouse ☐ Financial pressures ☐ Death of other close family member ☐ Serious personal injury or friend ☐ Serious injury or illness of family member ☐ Divorce or separation ☐ Change in career or job responsibility ☐ Moved your place of residence ☐ Other job difficulties
Question 3:	For the most part, do you tend to keep your feelings to yourself? ☐ Yes ☐ No
Question 4:	How often do you get physical exercise? ☐ Often ☐ Occasionally ☐ Seldom ☐ Never
Question 5:	Do you have a hobby? ☐ Yes ☐ No If yes, how often do you spend time on your hobby? ☐ Often ☐ Occasionally ☐ Seldom
Question 6:	Have you ever suffered from any of the following? (Check those which apply to you) ☐ Ulcers ☐ Hormonal problems ☐ Heart Disease ☐ High Blood Pressure ☐ Large weight gain or loss ☐ Sleep disturbances ☐ Migraine Headaches
Question 7:	Have you ever had cancer? ☐ Yes ☐ No If yes, what kind?_____
Question 8:	Have any of your relatives had cancer? ☐ Yes ☐ No ☐ Don't know If yes, what kind(s), if known?_____
Question 9:	Do you personally feel you have ever become ill because of stress? ☐ Yes ☐ No ☐ Undecided
Question 10:	Were you aware 3 out of 4 American families will be struck by cancer? ☐ Yes ☐ No
Question 11:	Will you help our effort to provide urgently needed funds to 45 promising cancer research projects and step up research in the area of stress-related cancer by making a contribution to the ⁚ ⁚ ⁚ Fund today? ☐ Yes ☐ No

I've enclosed my maximum contribution today in the amount of:

☐ **$15** ☐ **$25** ☐ **$50** ☐ **$100** ☐ **$250** ☐ **$500** ☐ **$_____ Other**

Mr. ⊃⁚ , please make your check payable to ARSVF.

SURVEY ON STRESS AND CANCER

Dear Friend,

Your answers are urgently needed on the enclosed 19 . Survey on Stress and Cancer especially registered in your name.

Did you know 3 out of every 10 Americans living today will eventually get cancer? More alarming, is about 50% of those who get it will die from the disease.

Perhaps you've been fortunate so far and cancer hasn't struck you or any of your family or friends.

We could only afford to send out Surveys today to a special group of key people like you across the country who we thought would be most interested in helping our nationwide study.

THIS IS IMPORTANT: EVEN IF YOU DO NOT WISH TO ANSWER YOUR SURVEY, OR ARE UNDECIDED ABOUT SOME SURVEY QUESTIONS, PLEASE RETURN IT TODAY IN THE POSTAGE PAID ENVELOPE.

This survey is costly to send out, and to get accurate results we must have yours back.

Your survey answers, when combined with others will help us find out how much you and others know about the stressful situations most closely linked with cancer.

Quite recently, cancer researchers have started to feel there may be a "cancer-prone" personality.

Our survey results could prove to be a valuable lead in research and education programs to help prevent the onset of cancer in literally thousands of Americans.

30

Please do these two things today, while it's fresh on your mind:

1) We urge you to complete and return your specially numbered
   Survey on Stress and Cancer in the postage paid envelope
   provided, so that we may tabulate your answers and forward
   them to researchers.

2) Enclose your maximum tax-deductible gift to ꞁꞁꞁꞁ for $15,
   $25, $50 or as much as you can afford to help us fund this
   and other promising cancer research projects. Even $10
   would be a big help.

We must be careful that we maximize every ꞁꞁ ꞁ dollar to cancer research
and we could only afford to send surveys to people like you who we thought
would be most interested in helping.

Remember, every 70 seconds another American dies of cancer. Our only
enemies are time and money. Please let us hear from you today.

Please join our efforts,

Your friends at the ꞁꞁꞁꞁ

P.S. Your survey is registered under your name here at ꞁꞁꞁ headquarters.
Even if you don't wish to answer it, we must have yours back to get accurate
results. We hope you will answer it and include a generous tax-deductible
gift to help us speed up promising cancer research projects.

SURVEY ON
STRESS AND CANCER

Enclosed Survey # 1075953

Assigned to:

Mr. Damo⌐ P ⌐ι
Box "
Williamsburg, VA   231'

Attention Williamsburg Postmaster:
Deliver contents to Box ꞁꞁꞁ only.

Post card.   Similar to the survey is the post card that the prospect is asked to mail to a significant individual. If you are raising funds for an emotional cause, why not include cards already addressed to a senator, the Attorney General, or another official who should consider the merits of your stand? These pre-addressed cards must carry a message strongly supporting the group's position on a significant issue.

This letter is a good illustration of the basic format.

My friend this is it...

    For the sake of your gun rights, mail the enclosed Postcards today.

    Your Postcards are needed in Washington, D.C., to help get Congress to pass the "McClure/Volkmer Firearms Owner Protection Act".

    Since 1968, when Congress passed the "Federal Gun Control Act", law-abiding gun owners and gun dealers have been harassed and intimidated by government agents.

    Just look at the fact sheet I'm enclosing. It is filled with stories of government intimidation of decent, law-abiding people like you and me.

    Now we have a chance to change that. But your help is needed to put the pressure on Congress to act before they adjourn around Labor Day.

    We already have 61 sponsors in the U.S. Senate. But we must get Senator Howard Baker, the Senate Majority Leader to schedule it for a vote.

    So mail the enclosed Postcards, now. One is to Senator Baker urging him to schedule the vote. Two Postcards are for your two U.S. Senators asking them to support the "Firearms Owner Protection Act". The Postcard for Senator McClure thanks him for his leadership on this important issue.

    Then please send me a $15 or $25 contribution to help me reach thousands of other gun owners with this Emergency Postcard Campaign.

A different concept — but the same technique — is used in this U.S.
Ski Team mailing.

**UNITED STATES SKI
EDUCATIONAL FOUNDATION**
P.O. BOX 4529
BOSTON, MASSACHUSETTS 02107

                              October 12, 19

Mr. John D. ѕamᵖₗe
ᵖsilᵢn Ⲅⲧa ⲁrᵍᵉmⲉnt
⸴. New Englⲁⲛⲋ
Burlinᵍ ., Massachusetts 018 .

Dear Mr. ѕamₚle:

        Do you think Becky Dorsey from Massachusetts, Jim
Denney or I can bring home top World Cup and World
Championship medals this year? You could hold the
answer.

        I know our whole Team has unlimited potential - but
we need help. You can become an Honorary Member of the
U.S. Ski Educational Foundation, the foundation that
supports the U.S. Ski Team. Your membership will help
provide the funds for training, medical care, and
everything else that makes the difference between winning
and losing.

        Competition this year will be tough. World Cup races
start in December, and the World Championships are in
February. We've got to be ready. We need your help
now to win all season long. Won't you become a member?

        And there's something else our Team needs from you.
When we're racing downhill at 70mph or putting in a
grueling 50 kilometers on a cross country course, it
helps us to know there are friends to wish us luck.

        Would you please let us all know that you support
us by mailing the enclosed postcard? I know my Teammates
would be thrilled to hear from you, and I would too.

        Look at the enclosed folder - it tells the special
awards available to you as an Honorary Member - Bronze,
Silver or Gold. Then please send your check to help us
today.

                         Sincerely,

                         Cindy Nelson

                         Cindy Nelson
                         U. S. Alpine Team

P.S. Our Jumping Team will be competing at Gunstock, NH
on January 20. I hope you'll plan to be there to cheer
them on.   *PARK CITY, UTAH — HOME OF THE U.S. SKI TEAM*

Sweepstakes. The publishing business developed sweepstakes to build response for book and magazine offers. They work with fund-raising, too. A sweepstakes, by appealing to a desire for riches, seems to smooth over the rough edges of difficult appeals, such as those for cancer research, or for the victims of blindness, deafness, retardation, or mental illness.

Before sending out a sweepstakes mailing, it is important to insure that certain legal requirements are met. Otherwise, you may end up running an illegal lottery. Be certain to consult your cause's legal counsel.

Also consider that, like strong medicines, sweepstakes may have unforeseen side effects. Some prospects object to them and will refuse to contribute. They can be complicated, expensive and controversial. Some board members may not be pleased at the thought that people are responding to win a prize rather than to support a cause. On the other hand, you will want to consider using a sweepstakes if you must raise money for something that is generally considered negative or difficult to understand and appreciate.

National Foundation for Cancer Research
7315 Wisconsin Avenue ■ Bethesda, Maryland 20014

Here's a gamble where everybody wins!

Our unique "laboratory without walls" links the work of scientists like Nobel Prize Winner, Dr. Albert Szent-Gyorgyi (shown here) in a unified war against cancer.

Dear Friend:

When a cancer research organization runs a sweepstakes, you can be sure of one thing: it needs money...and for an unexpected reason.

Our "unexpected reason" is simply this. We are making progress in developing a control for cancer faster than we anticipated.

Life itself is a gamble, and still it is worthwhile living! In life you can lose. Our sweepstakes is a gamble in which you can't lose.

The real grand prize is the possibility of a control for cancer. When you enter this sweepstakes, with a substantial tax-exempt contribution, you advance man's knowledge of cancer for sure. You may even save your loved ones from a painful death. And finally, you have a chance to win a valuable prize.

Of course, one can enter without enclosing a contribution. But that would be a set-back for cancer research.

Please help, and have fun. Just fill out the Sponsor's Certificate and return it along with the six attached sweepstakes entrance certificates...plus your gift. An addressed envelope is enclosed for your convenience.

                                        Thank you very much,

                                        Franklin C. Salisbury
                                        Executive Director

P.S. The National Foundation for Cancer Research isn't supported
      by taxes. We are totally dependent on tax-deductible dona-
      tions from concerned Americans like yourself. Even the prizes
      for this sweepstakes were contributed by friends of the
      Foundation.

Returnable check. In this involvement technique the prospect receives a signed check already made out to your organization. The letter explains that the check cannot be cashed unless its dollar amount is matched by an equivalent gift from the prospect, who must return your check with a matching contribution. This interesting concept has worked well, even though it is complicated enough to use up a sizeable portion of the fund-raising letter for an explanation. It is a novel idea that can turn a mediocre effort into a success story. It probably works so well because it simply isn't easy for the prospect to throw the original donor's check into the trash. That's the prime involvement element. It really looks like a check — printed on green check stock, with the amount printed in black and red, just as a check-writing machine would do.

Dear Friend:

A few months ago we received a sizable contribution from a donor with a condition attached to it. The condition was that we would have to at least double this contribution from the general public, or his contribution would not be valid.

He was aware of the continuing problem we have in meeting our research budget and the ever increasing cost due to inflation, and felt that this would be one way of stretching his dollars.

We thought about this challenge and wondered how we could accomplish it.

One of our staff came up with the suggestion of a matching check program similar to those which universities and other large nonprofit organizations use.

This sounded like a good idea and we immediately prepared it for mailing. It was a terrific success. People like you met the challenge and we more than doubled the original contribution.

It worked so well that we solicited other contributions with the same challenge attached. Many private foundations prefer to contribute funds with this kind of a challenge to the general public, and we have been successful in obtaining some grants.

So the checks included with this letter are being sent to you in hope that you will be able to meet this challenge. One check is for $10.00 and the other for $15.00. If you will match one or both, it will give our research effort a tremendous boost. You see, the check is made out to the ⟨illegible⟩ ⟨illegible⟩ and will not be deposited unless it is accompanied by another check of an equal amount or greater.

I do hope you will understand our needs and why we are resorting to this means of raising money. If we could double,

(over, please)

Take careful note of the material printed on the back of the matching donor's check. This prevents people from trying to cash the check for their personal use, and it keeps them from pestering the bank with queries about the appeal.

American Religious Vitality Society
MATCHING FUND ACCOUNT

May 3 19 ____

Pay to the
Order of   American Religious Vitality Society $ | 10.00

_____ Dollars

Manhattan Bank, N.A.
Philadelphia Pa. 191

This facsimile valid only if accompanied by
a donation check of equal or greater value.

H. Bitthason Lawrence

For deposit only
to the account of the
American Religious Vitality
Society

The Manhattan Bank, N.A.,
is a depository of funds only.
For further information about
this program, please write or
call the American Religious
Vitality Society.

The back of the check

Membership.   This is a tried and true approach to fund-raising. Its impact can be enhanced by offering variable membership levels and benefits. Benefits may include anything from glossy magazines to discounts at gift shops, walnut plaques and even jewelry. Several groups offer major donors a toll-free "for members only" telephone number to use in contacting their officials. In the United States, the membership dues are actually a contribution of sorts, but only part of those dues are tax-deductible — the amount that exceeds the value of the benefits. Members are usually asked to make gifts in addition to their dues contributions. They become excellent annual giving prospects, for example. Here, a hospital offers attractive benefits to prospects who become charter members of a new Associates program. The dues contribution is low, but possibly can be raised when the group becomes established.

I am writing today and asking you to join us in something entirely new and very worthwhile.

Accepting this invitation can mean that you, or someone in your family, will feel better and live longer. That certainly is a major benefit, isn't it? So act now and take advantage of today's health care progress at ·.·.·.·.·.· Hospital. Accept this Charter Membership in our Associates program and give us your support.

You'll find your personal Charter Member number is already printed on the enclosed reply form. All you need do to accept is return the form with your tax-deductible contribution to the hospital. You'll become a supporter of medical progress and at the same time gain some very worthwhile benefits.

Member Benefits Are Available Both Night and Day!

They include:

a) Your personal, embossed Charter Member's Card

This card bears a 24 hour telephone number which you are invited to use at any time of the day or night. Imagine the peace of mind you will have by knowing that if anyone in your family should become ill, or injured, you have a handy number to call for assistance. That's not all! You'll find a special members' service number for use with your other worthwhile benefits.

b) Special Pre-Registration Privileges (if you wish)

Accept this offer and your immediate family will not have delays when referred here by your physician or

P.S. Here's what your contribution brings you in the way of membership benefits:

Contribute	You Receive
$10	Embossed Annual Member Card with 24 hour emergency number, special number for member services and your own pre-registration or recognition number
	Pre-registration privileges
	Special I.D. bracelet (if patient)
	Informative newsletter
$25	(all benefits above) PLUS "Wish a Friend Well Program" and Children's Special Welcome Program
$50	(all benefits above) PLUS invitation to Annual Dinner and embossed certificate
$100	(all benefits above) PLUS discounted television service and FREE parking.

Premiums. An "up front" premium is something sent with the gift solicitation — such items as address labels, key rings, or inexpensive pens. You must be careful with your selection of an up-front premium. They often seem to arrive as "unordered merchandise," and many people send nothing or only a token amount as a gift. Small contributions frequently make up the bulk of response — not what most fund-raisers want. One "up front" premium that sometimes is effective is a temporary membership card. Because it has no intrinsic value, it does not annoy prospects as merchandise may. Another effective up-front premium is your group's decal, and a request that the prospect support your cause by pasting it on his or her car or window. Deciding to display your decal is already a significant form of involvement for a prospect. The contribution is an easy next step.

Premiums also can be offered in your appeal letter, to be sent in recognition of a gift, but only after the gift is made. The U.S. Ski Team has offered gold and silver costume jewelry to donors. Lapel pins are effective, partly because recipients want to be recognized by others who believe as they do. Large gifts may merit a walnut plaque, distinctive luggage tags, embossed membership cards, and a broad range of special privileges. One symphony orchestra has offered classical recordings, free admission to specified rehearsal concerts, music lectures, and meeting invitations. Zoological parks offer free parking, free admissions, publications, tickets to a children's zoo, and free tramway rides.

Your imagination is the only limit to the premiums you offer. The only requirements are a low "bottom-line" cost and the ability to raise your prospect's involvement in your appeal. Here, a university offers alumni an imaginative, desirable and low-cost up-front premium — a card you fill in to get back in touch with your long-lost classmate.

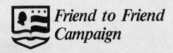

Friend to Friend Campaign

September 27, 19

Dear Alum,

Where are the friends we sat in class with, studied with, worried and dreamed with, shared laughter and tears with...?

Those important people who were a major part of our lives during our years at GWU, may have been lost through the years. But our Friend to Friend campaign can help you locate your friends and classmates and renew those relationships that made your college days at GWU so special.

To locate your classmate, simply fill in the enclosed Friend to Friend card and return it to us. All we need is the name, school and year of graduation of the friend you wish to contact. We will forward the card with your personal message to your classmate's current address. Remember to include your name, address and phone number so your friend can contact you after receiving the card.

As you renew your personal friendships I ask you to renew your friendship with the University through a contribution to the 19 - ˉ Annual Fund.

Your gift of any amount, $100, $50, $25 is especially meaningful this year. As you know, GW was awarded an $800,000 Challenge Grant from the

CONSIDER PERSONALIZING THE LETTER

The more personal a letter appears, the more effective it will probably be in raising funds. The ideal — difficult to reach — is for the prospect to feel as if someone in your cause sat down and wrote a letter just to him or her. This is why a sound knowledge of the market — prospects and their attitudes — is essential. The more you know about your prospects and donors, and the more of this data you maintain in an accessible form in your computer, the more direct and personal your appeal can become. For some fund-raisers, personalization means putting the prospect's name and address at the top of the letter and using the prospect's name in the salutation. For others, these and other elements are also worked into the letter's text: "you and your neighbors on *Edgewood Drive*..." But there are even more effective ways to personalize.

Computer letters.   The computer, used imaginatively, offers a broader range of personalization than simple fill-ins. Computer letters allow a huge number of variable pieces of information to be custom-assembled for each prospect. Among variables worth considering are geographic area, street address, size of last gift, date of last gift, total gifts to date, graduation year, known interests, date of birth, names of nearby contributors, name and location of local chapter, local chapter officers, telephone numbers, and just about anything else you would naturally include in a letter to a friend.

Writing a computer letter does not mean that you have to flaunt personalization constantly. The temptation is to overuse personalization and thereby make it appear artificial and forced. Repeating a person's name several times is hardly the height of sophistication. True, most of us enjoy seeing our own name. Yet seeing it too often seems to create a feeling of alarm in all but the most benighted egotists.

Some copywriters like to start off with a bang: "I'm wondering why I haven't heard from you since last April when you generously sent *$15* to help us *care for Jimmy and the other boys.*" Others find it more natural to work the personalizations into later paragraphs. To save money, many computer letters have only the first page personalized. Sometimes a four-page letter will have the first and last pages personalized and the two middle pages printed to match. (The trick then is to get all your personalization into half the letter without losing, in the other half, the personal, friendly touch that brings in donors and dollars.)

When you, the letter-writer, are composing a letter for computer personalization, you simply have to write it differently than you would a "Dear Friend" letter. You must keep the reader's perception in mind. If the reader picks up a "Dear Friend" letter, it's immediately clear that the text was in no way composed for just one person. But the computer letter — with its capacity for "Dear *Slim*" salutations, and references to "your dog, *Nero*" — must sound as if the whole text were written for one, known person: Slim. If not — if you write a "your husband or wife" text that's applicable to millions, and then drop in computer-generated "Dear *Slim*" and "your dog, *Nero*" references — you will have created a rather obvious split-personality effect. The reader will smell a rat — an insincere rat. This is an effect that may disturb or confuse your reader rather than one that will inspire him or her to a generous gift.

How do you do it? Well, it's all a matter of "mental set." You must work out in your mind the kind of communications situation you're in. What is your role? What is the prospect's role? What "voice" do you use, and what is your relationship with the prospect? If it's a computer letter, you might ask yourself: "What would I say if this were just one letter that I was writing to this one person? How would I sound? What words would I use? What would I say if I were to call this one person and make the appeal by phone?"

Here are some fairly standard computer personalizations that may
be useful.

- Include the name of the prospect's town or state.

along with other leaders in the Clarksburg community, I'm
inviting you to join many informed Ohio voters who have

- Use specifics to ask for an upgraded gift.

so please try and send $60, or at least $45, as you did
last year.

- Use specifics to point out how long the donor has supported you.

Your wonderful help, beginning back in 1982, has
made a real difference. You'll probably recognize

- Use the prospect's name in the P.S.

P.S. Believe me, Mr. Jones, your support means a
       great deal to me personally.

This kind of personalization, if properly used, will enhance results. You also can calculate exactly how much it will raise your production and mailing costs. So you can easily determine how much increased response will be required to make the additional investment for personalization pay off. If you are after major donors and expect average gifts of $50 or more, perhaps even $1,000 and over, your rate of response will ordinarily be rather low. A handful of additional checks received per thousand letters mailed can make a substantial improvement in results. On the other hand, if you are after the donor who sends anywhere from $5 to $25, personalization may not pay for itself. This is simply because profits from the increased response will probably be insufficient to defray the considerable increase in production costs.

As a rule of thumb, you can figure that personalization is worthwhile when mailing to your donor list and probably to former donors. With them, you are in a position to mention the size of their last gift, when it was made, and how it was used. Therefore you can write a truly effective personal letter to a group of people whose expected rate of response is high.

By the same rule of thumb, unless you are after a very small response with a very high average gift and are using tested prospect lists, heavy personalization will usually not pay its way when writing to non-donors.

Fill-ins. With today's technology, there is a less expensive middle ground. You can take a printed letter and then, using a computer, type in the prospect's name, address and salutation — and perhaps even more — in a way that perfectly matches the printing. If you do it right, only an expert will suspect the ''fill-ins'' of being done separately. This technique is often used when a full computer-generated letter would be too expensive.

The most typical fill-in is done by using a computer or automatic typewriter to insert the inside name, address and salutation. But it is also possible to put similar inserts, such as a person's name, state of residence, or any other variable, directly in the letter text. This can present problems, of course: If the insert is too high, too low, lopsided, or has any other flaw, it will then subtract rather than add to the effectiveness of your mailing piece. By sticking just to the name, address, and salutation, slightly faulty registration will probably not be noticeable.

Personalized salutations.   "Dear Friend" is generally used with printed letters. But even this can be personalized a bit. "Dear Conservationist," "Dear Parent," "Dear Haverford Alumnus," "Dear Concerned Citizen," "Dear Music Lover," and the like will at least show your prospect that you are aware of his or her relationship to your organization.

Way back in the Big Band Era of the 1930's, a then popular song insisted, "It's not what you do, but the way that you do it — That's what gets results." And this refrain fits direct-mail fund-raising well. As has already been pointed out, the style and language of your fund-raising appeal will definitely influence its success.

The basic fault of many who seek to write fund-raising mailing packages is a disease known as egotism. Board chairmen, physicians, attorneys, fund-raising executives, and others are often more concerned with their own images than with contributions. The letters they compose are used to advertise their astuteness, vocabulary, social prominence, or whatever — all at the expense of the charitable group for which contributions are solicited.

Direct-mail is a high-cost medium. Such things as a patronizing tone of voice, complicated syntax, multisyllabic words, and overlong paragraphs should be viewed as vicious attacks on the "bottom line." They steal funds from the cause's basic mission. How do you avoid such mistakes?

Always take an objective view of your fund-raising. Remember that, while the cause may be important to you and your colleagues, it may not loom as essential to everyone who receives your mailings. Many prospects may consider your fund-raising letter as "junk mail," a nuisance by definition. They will read it only if you make your appeal obviously worthwhile — worthwhile by their values, not by yours. It must also appear sincere, easy to understand and simple to act upon. Most newspapers are written in words that are understandable to a ninth-grade student. When one considers that a daily newspaper generally is read by the better educated segments of the population, it becomes obvious that an effective fund-raising letter absolutely must use simple words that most Americans readily comprehend.

Much to the surprise of some self-styled intelligentsia, writing effective, basic English is never easy. It is actually more difficult to write something that is clear and easy to understand than it is to write something that appears erudite. The successful writer of fund-

3 FRI

raising letters must convey even the most difficult message in terms that are readily comprehended and can be instantly grasped and acted upon. The following points are especially significant.

Think short.   A solid page of type *appears* difficult to read. Your prospects are not being paid to work at reading your letter. Why should they bother with a difficult-appearing text? They have no obligation to do so. You would like them to join the cause? Then, you will have to convince them first that it's okay to read your letter. Short, simple sentences and paragraphs break up the page and make it look easy to read. Try expressing only a single thought in each sentence; it will make it easy to keep your sentences short.

Just looking at the next letter — an early draft — is enough to make a strong person quail. The message may be interesting but reading it appears to be very hard work.

>   Action on Smoking and Health (ASH) has prepared this presentation to help employers appreciate both the immediate and long-range economic benefits of implementing "quit smoking" programs for smoking employees, and of establishing policies to protect nonsmoking employees from exposure to tobacco in the workplace. Today private business firms are expressing more interest than ever before in smoking cessation programs for their employees. In one month ASH has received in excess of 60 separate company requests for assistance and/or information on how to reduce smoking among employees.
>
>   These companies writing for our suggestions have already realized the fact that smoking is bad business. One fifth of all lost work days in the U.S. is attributable to the effects of cigarette smoking;[1] a 2-pack-a-day smoker is absent from work 150% more often than a nonsmoker.[2] Cigarettes are a major cause of damage to furniture[3] and carpets, the leading ignition source for small fires,[4] and a prime cause of damage to inventory and expen-

Here is how it was rewritten.

> Action on Smoking and Health has received more than 60 requests asking how smoking among company employees may be reduced to protect the health of non-smokers and cut down on illness and absenteeism.
>
> These companies are among a growing number which find that smoking is bad business. They have read statistics pointing out that 20% of lost work days are attributable to cigarettes, and that smoking injures furniture, carpets, damages equipment, and greatly increases medical and disability payments. Therefore, smoking also contributes towards higher insurance costs.
>
> Along with these negative economic aspects of smoking, employers now find that smoking causes discomfort among non-smoking employees and customers.

Long, convoluted streams of thought don't succeed. Short sentences containing single thoughts and easy-to-understand words are essential. Here is part of a long, two-page letter. It's broken up into short sentences and paragraphs. It provides a great deal of information, along with some emotion, in a non-frightening format.

When Dr. Barney B. Clark

Volunteered for an Artificial Heart

We Had Already Tested It for Years

On a Variety of Animals...

...yet, as you have seen and heard from news reports, his Jarvik VII artificial heart had serious limitations. It required a drive system on wheels the size of a shopping cart that was by his side the rest of his life.

We must do better! That is why I am inviting you to join in support of research on the artificial heart.

First, here's something you should know:

The goal of artificial heart research is NOT useless prolongation of life. Sure you agree that life without health and mobility is more burden than blessing.

Speak of short sentences! Look at the length of the first paragraph of this next letter. But it works! It interests the reader into going on to the next paragraph, which leads easily into the third paragraph, where the reader is asked for a gift. The writing style is relaxed. The prospect's name is worked into the fourth paragraph in a natural, easy way. The writer isn't simply demonstrating that his cause has a new computer.

November 5

Mr. John D ⎽⎽⎽
⎽⎽ l⎽ ⎽⎽⎽a ⎽
⎽⎽ New ⎽r lan
Burl⎽ ⎽g⎽ ⎽, Massachusetts 018⎽

Dear John:

I'm worried.

When something bothers me I write you. It makes me
feel better. And I know I can count on you to help me.

I am writing you this letter to ask if you can send a
special Christmas gift of $35. I desperately need your
help.

You see, John, I just don't have enough money to get
us through the Winter.

I've checked and rechecked our records--and we are
already dangerously low on money. As you know, our expenses are highest during the Winter months.

Fuel bills, winter clothes, school needs and other
big expenses face us. And I've already done everything
I can. I've cut budgets, mended old clothes--anything to

50

Here is a powerful first sentence that quickly transforms a national problem into a very local challenge. The gift is not to keep the program on the air; it's to keep it on the air *in the prospect's own hometown.* Notice the short sentences, each with a single thought. Also, notice the short paragraphs and the generous use of white space.

September 3, 19

Mr. Christopher W. B..t
.5" t.J- /c Drive
Ambler, Pennsylvania 1900..

Dear Mr. B.]t.. s. ':

    I urgently need your help to keep the Word of God Hour on the air in Ambler.

    As I mentioned to you last month, rising costs may force us to lose several stations around the country.

    It would be a shame if you tuned in Channel 2 -- and some cartoon or ungodly program was there in place of the Word of God Hour.

    But that can happen!

    And then what about persons like the dear friend I told you about whose husband was saved -- during our program -- just two days before he died?

Speak the prospect's language. Together with being clear, your message should convey that you, the writer, are part of "their crowd." This is not a problem when addressing the general public. But it becomes more difficult when an appeal involves a unique audience such as conservationists, cancer patients, alumni of a specific college, or others who communicate with one another in a special vocabulary.

Colonial Williamsburg, for example, has its own way of saying things. This letter is intentionally "stuffy." The audience consists of well-to-do people who either have Colonial forebears, or wish they had them. Not every organization can refer to its donors as "distinguished fellow citizens," as does the last paragraph shown here.

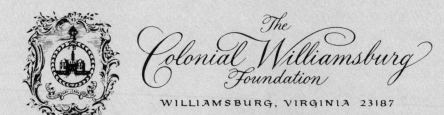

Office of the President

"We hold these truths to be self evident;
that all men are created equal; that they
are endowed by their creator with certain
unalienable rights; that among these are
life, liberty, and the pursuit of happiness."

THOMAS JEFFERSON

The words ring clearly down through the centuries as
part of our Declaration of Independence.

They were borrowed, almost verbatim, from the Virginia
Bill of Rights presented to the House of Burgesses here in
Williamsburg by Mr. Jefferson's good friend, George Mason.

For here is where much of America began when Patrick
Henry, George Mason, Thomas Jefferson, George Washington, and
their fellow patriots decided to risk everything, including
their lives, for freedom.

Today, more than two hundred years later, the freedoms
our forebears won remain only a dream for most of humanity. You
and I are fortunate. We inherited the right to speak our minds
freely, elect our own government, and receive equal justice
under law.

I expect you agree these priceless rights deserve more
recognition and better understanding. That is why I am writing
this letter and inviting you to join with other distinguished
fellow citizens in support of Colonial Williamsburg.

You cannot simply insert a few "code words" to demonstrate that
you are an insider. They must appear natural. Otherwise you convey the impression that you are salting a mine with precious stones.

There is nothing like religion when it comes to special vocabulary, but in this letter it seems natural.

Christmas Greetings

Dear Friend,

The wonderful Christmas season is here again. Yet for millions of Americans, Christmas 19?? has about it a gloom and a sadness. The crisis at home and abroad will not go away! In October, as events piled one upon another in the Middle East, it seemed that the world went to the brink of Armageddon.

Our Lord predicted, "And there shall be signs in the sun, and in the moon, and in the stars; and upon the earth distress (to be pressed from all sides) of nations with

Now the "will of man" runs riot in the earth. Then the "will of the Lord" will alone be done. Isaiah prophesied, "The Lord alone shall be exalted in that day" (Isaiah 2:17).

Till that time we are under orders from the King of Kings to proclaim His message. He prophesied, "And this gospel of the Kingdom shall be preached in all the world for a witness unto all nations, and then shall the end come." When we engage in evangelism, we are obeying His great command "to go and proclaim." In doing so we are also hastening the day of His return.

Contractions are another point to consider. While a few tend to make an appeal more friendly, too many may weaken the overall impact. So throw in a few contractions where they seem to fit best. In this computer-personalized letter, young Cindy clearly is right in saying "I'm upset."

```
                                  Cindy McSpeaker
                                  460 Mitchell Drive
                                  Seattle, Washington 98112


     Mr. Christopher V. ᴖalt᷀ᷞ᷀⸱
     .5. Edgewood Drive
     Ambler, Pennsylvania 190ᴖ᷀

     Dear Mr. ᴖalt᷀ᷞ᷀:

          My name is Cindy McSpeaker and I live here in Seattle,
     Washington where I am a student at Sidkoff Junior High
     School.

          I'm writing you because I'm upset that so many
     teen-agers like me (I'm 15) are wrecking their lives
     with drugs and turning against the Bible, their parents
     and their country.

          Chances are you know or have heard of teen-agers
     around Edgewood Drive, or in Ambler, who are like that.
```

Brighten your vocabulary.   The writers of effective letters forget about being self-important, and write in the easiest, friendliest way that they can. It is sincerity and a friendly interest that produce money. Pontificating turns people off. People don't want to be "told," or preached too. They want to know how your cause impacts on them, what it means to them personally, how it may change their lives or the lives of their loved ones, and why giving to it is in the donor's self interest.

Writers who are obsessed with their *own* self interest generally cannot write effective fund-raising appeals. So, the first step in brightening your vocabulary is a psychological one; you must stop writing for and about yourself and start concentrating on writing for your reader. To do this, you must get to know your reader. Go out and actually meet a cross section of your donors. Visit them in their homes. Attend functions held for them. Scan your donor lists to see what kinds of people are on it. Lots of single women? People being addressed at their businesses? People with titles like ''Dr.,'' or ''The Hon.''? Home addresses in simple neighborhoods? Well-to-do neighborhoods? In short, get a ''feel'' for the kind of person who contributes to your cause and their reasons for giving. Then, in your mind, write to *that* person.

If you are successful in doing this, your vocabulary will change automatically. If it doesn't, force it to. Stop using ''I,'' and begin using ''you.'' ''I'' is the worst word you can use. Why should your prospects care about your cause's needs and concerns? They have enough of their own. Show the prospect how your cause affects him or her. Why should such topics as space exploration, apartheid, Communist infiltration in Central America, or finding answers to Alzheimer's disease, concern the prospects? They're more wrapped up in exploration of ways to lower car and mortgage payments, the need for a new freezer, a concern about the roof, or political situations in the office. Your job is to expand their horizons — to convince them that, unless they contribute to stop drunk drivers, someone they love may be killed by one . . . that, if bald eagles vanish because of pollution, their own children may be next . . . that, unless the right candidates win the upcoming elections, their dental practice may be on the rocks.

Dear Dr. amᵢ ˋ ˙:

    Your private practice and our profession are in jeopardy. The facts are in your daily newspaper. That's why we must take action now.

    With the pressures of national health programs, the spread of illegal dentistry and the increasing control of federal regulatory agencies, your personal involvement is of vital importance.

    Please join many of your colleagues throughout Texas who are contributing to the Texas ⟨illegible⟩ Committee. ⟨illegible⟩ supports candidates who believe in the best oral health care and understand the importance of professional dental care. We know that unless our friends win seats in Congress and state legislatures, we risk the election of those who would destroy all that you and I believe in and have worked so hard for.

    We're off to a fine start. Dr. ⟨illegible⟩ says 91% of ⟨illegible⟩'s candidates for the last session won. But we must make sure our voice is heard in both state and national elections. We cannot

The more unobtrusive your own ego becomes, the more effective your appeal will be. This is one of the most difficult aspects of letter-writing to accomplish. It is often what separates the professionals from the amateurs. You may encounter this difference when dealing with a board member or other letter-signer who wants to flaunt his or her ego in an appeal. When that happens, rewrite the text.

Edit the ego out, and restore the "you" element.

Remember, your performance will mainly be gauged by whether or not the mailing raises money. And this is accomplished by "you," not by "I."

Use "action" words — words that bring your scenario to vivid life. "Smash" drug-dealing. "Conquer" cancer. "March" for peace. Use "image-conveying" words like: "starvation," "torture," "rags," or "disease." Look at the impact that just two words — "sadistic parents" — create in this appeal for a children's home.

```
    You've been a good friend to our children.  That's why I
want to tell you about little four year old Beth.

    To you, Beth's story could sound unreal.  Neglected and
beaten by sadistic parents, forced to live on garbage, she cried
herself to sleep each night.

    Out of concern for her life, Beth was rescued by grand-
parents and brought to
```

Vary your words. Unless it's used for dramatic effect, repetition is boring. Using the same nouns, verbs, adjectives, and constructions over and over again will turn off your prospects.

While you're writing, you probably won't notice if you're overusing certain words or phrases. You discover it later when you read back what you've written — preferably after getting away from the text for an hour or so, even a day or so.

If you get stuck and feel your vocabulary is limited, turn to a thesaurus or dictionary for help. Such reference books can provide substitute words, easily and quickly. Is yours an "important" appeal addressing an "important" problem for an "important" cause? Why not a "deadly" problem and a "crucial" appeal? They're all in the reference books. In writing, as in music, varied themes and combinations stand the test of time.

Use punctuation for meaning. Successful fund-raising is emotional. Emotion may be assisted by clever use of punctuation that emphasizes significant points and changes the look of your letter. Here are some ideas for you to consider.

- Use double dashes (--) to mark phrases in apposition instead of the usual commas. If not overdone, this opens up your sentence and creates more white space.

```
The objective -- as always -- is to make your
copy seem easy to read.
```

- Employ triple dots, or even more dots, to add continuity. Once again we are using white space creatively, breaking up our page and making reading it appear less of a chore.

```
He raced home...shaved...showered...rushed
into the kitchen.
```

- In the next letter, the punctuation of the headline, the exclamation points in the last paragraph shown, the dashes in the paragraph above that — all these illustrate how punctuation may emphasize the meaning of the message.

International Shooter Development Fund
P.O. Box 37439
Washington, D.C. 20013

Get this special
limited edition,
U.S. Shooting Team
Patch...

...AND get your
chance to win an
instant collection
of America's finest
firearms!

Dear Friend,

Because you are an NRA member and a supporter of the shooting sports, you now have the opportunity to win some of the greatest firearms made in America today:

A Ruger "Red Label" Over and Under 20 Gauge Shotgun

A Colt Python .357 Magnum Revolver

A Winchester Model 9422 Lever Action Rimfire Rifle

A Remington Model 700 "Classic" 7mm Magnum Rifle

A Smith & Wesson Model 41 .22 Target Auto-Loading Pistol

The entire collection -- one of each of the finest firearms of their type -- has a total retail value of over $3,000.

And it could all be yours! The entire collection! Just for entering the U.S. SHOOTING TEAM All-American Great Guns Sweepstakes today.

- Use underlines and brackets for special emphasis. The effect can be powerful, especially if you make the additional elements look like handwriting and print them in another color, as was done in this example. Too much of this kind of emphasis can make your letter look heavy and complex. But just the right amount can produce positive results. (A technical note: With computer-generated letters, underlining can present a production problem. One solution is to locate beforehand exactly where the underlined word will appear and to print the underlining along with your letterhead before the computer text is run.)

This program has a dual purpose. Of course the major goal is to help those who cannot hear. Imagine what it must mean to live in total silence unable to understand the voices of one's loved ones.

(Just imagine a mother unable to hear her baby cry, a child oblivious to an approaching truck, or an elderly person who doesn't realize the doorbell is ringing or the smoke sensor is activated!)

So far, thirty-two Hearing Dogs have been placed. We have 13 million partially deaf people in this country; 2 million more are totally deaf! Much remains to be done and we are trying to expand the program to answer an immense demand.

I'm asking for your financial support because funds are urgently needed to continue this program. Each dog's training costs approximately $1,800 and they are placed at no cost to the deaf.

Every Hearing Dog is "custom" trained by American Humane for the specific needs of the deaf person with whom it will be living. Any dog that might fail training will be placed with elderly persons seeking companion dogs.

It's really rather wonderful! The deaf are able to "hear"

The Hearing Dog Program

- To emphasize thoughts, use handwritten notes as post-scripts, or at the top of your text, or as annotations in the margins. Once again, too much can be a mistake; it can interfere with the smooth flow of your text and clutter up the page. But if they're used carefully and logically, such notes can make a complicated issue easier to understand or drive home points that would otherwise take a far longer letter to explain fully. Done right, the technique also makes the computer letter look very, very much like an individually typed and annotated piece of correspondence.

This example uses a handwritten note printed by offset on a computer-generated follow-up, carbon-copy mailing. It gives new life to a message that may have been seen once before . . . and ignored.

Make grammar work for you. With few exceptions, effective fund-raising letters employ good grammar. Using good grammar lets an audience relax and pay attention to what you are saying — instead of being distracted by the way you say it.

Good grammar alone will not produce additional response or dollars for a fund-raiser. On the other hand, poor grammar and clearly wrong punctuation, when directed towards educated prospects or donors, might have a negative impact.

What is "good grammar"? Some letter-writers do not seem to understand the difference between a phrase and a sentence. Others drop in commas and semicolons without understanding the difference between them. The rules are not mysterious. Grammar and punctuation guides can be bought at almost every bookstore. If your questions become more subtle and aim at style, then "The New York Times Manual of Style and Usage" is a good, standard guide. It's the stylebook used by the editors and writers of The New York Times.

Having people understand you is the first basic step in writing any fund-raising letter. While a few widely used colloquialisms may make a letter less formal and more easily read, there is no substitute for proper phrasing and sentence construction.

This doesn't mean you should be stuffy. It means (the same idea again) you should keep your reader in mind. It means that you must use what the reader will see as reasonably good manners. Many people look on poor grammar as bad manners. It offends them. You cannot afford to offend anyone who might mail back a check.

On the other hand, if the usage fits, it's perfectly safe to use flagrantly ungrammatical constructions in your fund-raising letter (although your board may cringe when you do). It's okay to write things like: "You ain't seen nothing yet!"; "What did he do that for?"; or "You'll have to more than double your gift." (The New York Times, which counsels that you should generally avoid a split infinitive, says the last example actually is "justified" because you're working with a compound verb and adverb.) In fact, such constructions can give a liveliness and humanity to your letter that make it more interesting, more convincing.

In short, if you break the rules of grammar, punctuation, or style, do it on purpose and for a reason — a reason that will produce more gift income.

Use criticism creatively.   You may know the sinking feeling that comes when the text you have toiled over is torn apart by critics: the boss, the board, the lawyer, or some obnoxious presence. While kicking office furniture, or throwing a tantrum at home may release tension, it is not an effective answer to such criticism. Rather, here are the *sensible* ways to proceed.

- Sit quietly and consider whether you should really go back to your typewriter. Maybe they're right. Sometimes a letter that looks wonderful to you when first written will appear less exciting a few days later. Generally speaking, a day or so of reflection followed by a rewrite will make a good mailing piece even better.

- Consider the source. If the criticism comes from someone who understands direct-mail fund-raising, perhaps you should listen. On the other hand, if you believe the comments have no real merit, you have a selling job to do. You will have to explain why you wrote as you did — why it is the most effective way to proceed — and perhaps to provide proof from expert witnesses or from earlier tests.

- Ask for a new test mailing. Testing is expensive, but it leads to greater net profits in the long run. If you are convinced the critics are in error, a fair test is the best way to prove it.

- Recognize that practically every large mailing will produce some negative replies. Some come from people who are against your cause. Some come from people who misunderstand your letter and assume things you have not said. Some are from fervent anti-advertisers or ''anti-junk-mail'' indivduals. Some are from the obvious mental cases. You may even receive a few sincere, well thought out responses that question your organization's ethics, ask why you are spending money on fund-raising that should go directly to needy recipients, or contradict some of the points you have made.

The major problem arises when board members and directors become aware of the negative replies and fail to realize that they are very few when considered as a percentage of the total mailing. Sometimes negative replies are used against your direct-mail program by those who opposed mailings in the first place. Gripes written to board members by personal friends are the most damaging of all.

The answer to all this hubbub is very simple. Define your objectives, point out exactly what you have done to achieve them, and explain the results. The best answer can be stated in two words: ''It works!''

If you can also show that the objections received are greatly out-numbered by contributions — as is generally the case — so much the better. If negative responses can be considered votes against your program, then gift checks can be considered votes in favor. Focus your cause's attention on those positive votes. Most board members are sensible human beings, dedicated to the goals of your organization. Negative responses may even end up serving a positive purpose. They can give you a chance to explain your mailing goals fully — what you have done and why you did it in a certain way — to the very people who need that sort of education.

Know yourself. Writing is a creative process, offering all the blessings and problems associated with creativity. No two creative people seem to go about the process in the same way. Yet people who have become good at creating things have one characteristic in common: They know themselves. They know what triggers creativity in themselves.

So you should be on the lookout for this same insight into yourself.

There may be as many writing systems as there are writers. My own is very simple. I simply roll paper into my typewriter and begin. The important thing for me is to get started. If you don't know what to say, just write down the first thought that comes to mind. Don't waste time worrying about "writer's block." Just sit down, think of a friend, or someone you like, and begin writing him or her a letter. You can't do it? Oh, yes, you can. Begin with any thought that comes to mind. "How are you?" "What's new?" "It's been a while since I wrote you last." "There's something I'd like to tell you about."

It is always a good idea to have some sort of check list of the important points you must cover. Having the list in front of you makes it easy to slip the key points into the text wherever there's a natural opening. That way, they'll all eventually get into your letter.

Don't attempt to create a finished piece of fund-raising copy as your first draft. It's sure to be ineffective. Figure that your initial effort is going to be only a rough sketch. A portrait painter generally roughs out ideas with charcoal on a pad . . . then goes on canvas with a more refined sketch . . . and gradually, even before the first splash of paint, the finished result starts to take shape in the artist's mind. A letter also needs a rough outline, a bit of refining, and then the polishing that will produce maximum impact and results.

When beginning a letter, I don't even consider how long the finished piece is supposed to be. My system, if you want to call it that, consists of working fairly quickly at first to get my rough outline down on paper; and then slowing down to become more exacting and critical with every line, and even with each individual word in its context.

After completing a rough outline, I look it over, edit it . . . check to see that all important ideas are included . . . and use it as a guide from which to rewrite. Sometimes it takes a half dozen rewrites before the result even begins to resemble a good piece for fund-raising.

Sooner or later, though, the letter more or less comes together. Now is the time to consider the opening sentence, to study the text paragraph by paragraph, to see how effectively the various points on your list are being stressed.

Consider the "sequence" with an extremely critical eye. What should come first? Which paragraph should follow? Will changing the paragraph sequence produce a more logical or emotional result? Have you asked for support in the first two or three paragraphs — making sure the reader realizes why you are sending him or her this particular appeal?

One thing I always check at this time is whether eliminating the first one or two paragraphs will strengthen my letter. Often a writer's original openings are weak, but lead into something much stronger. You cannot afford a weak opening. So spot your strongest lead paragraph — the one that will force the reader to continue — and move it to the lead.

Then I consider the mechanical problems. Computer personalization usually is responsible for most of these. A certain phrase *must* appear at a specific place on the page. Personalization can only be done on certain pages. One introduction must serve for several different personalized computer fill-ins. All of these mechanical considerations must be met — always with the text looking unforced and natural.

Spend time on your closing. I personally find that a fast call for action is the best way to close. "Make your sale and leave quickly," is the best rule to follow in a letter, just as it is in a personal visit.

Obviously it isn't easy to get your letter into final shape. It generally pays to take a fund-raising piece you feel is almost ready and to set it aside for a day, or at least overnight. Then, when you return to it again, you will often quickly see ways of improving your impact. I've heard that letters can be over-polished. Frankly, I find this unbelievable. Most pieces of fund-raising copy will benefit from additional work. The polishing can go on forever. Deadlines usually prevent appeals from being as good as they might have been. But there does come a point where changing a word or a phrase really will not make a difference in dollar results. I don't know exactly where that point is, and neither does anyone else. That is why testing is so important. In fund-raising letters, what works most profitably is not a matter of opinion, but rather a matter of hard cold statistical evidence.

I've told you how I manage to get myself moving on a fund-raising letter. Now it's time to study yourself and to find the system that brings you to your optimum peak of creativity. It's worth doing, because tapping your full creative potential is one of the most vital keys to writing a solid gold fund-raising letter.

There are no absolutes in fund-raising by mail. Some letters that ignore basic rules are enormously successful. But nonetheless, it helps to know the rules, so here are the least controversial.

THE RIGHT WAY TO BEGIN

If the opening paragraph fails to involve your audience, an expensive letter may end its life in the trash. But you can avoid that.

Some successful fund-raisers strive to start their letters by agreeing with their prospects' outlook. The objective is to get them nodding along in agreement so that the appeal for a gift, when it comes, also will be agreed to almost automatically.

However you do it, one objective must be to get the prospective donor's attention and interest as quickly as possible. Devices regularly used for this purpose include asking a question, offering a poignant quotation, stating a position, or describing a situation. Let's look at examples of each.

- A question — from a little girl

4

RP Foundation
Children have so much to see.
And they should all have a chance to see it.

"Mommy, Why Is This Happening To Me?"

How do you explain to your little girl that she is going blind, and there is no treatment or cure? How do you keep from crying when she can no longer see well enough to skip rope and romp with her little friends?

Tracy is 9 years old. She lives in Rome, Georgia, and has Retinitis Pigmentosa (RP), an inherited disease which attacks children and young people. Its cause is unknown. Although inherited, it may vanish for generations and then suddenly reappear.

As I write you today RP is incurable. That's why I'm asking you for help. Each additional day that passes without a cure means more girls and boys are going blind.

67

- A quotation — by a native American

Director
John E. Echohawk

Deputy Director
Thomas W. Fredericks

Attorneys
Joseph J. Brecher
Walter R. Echo-Hawk
David H. Getches
Roy S. Haber
Daniel H. Israel
Yvonne T. Knight
Scott E. Little
Douglas R. Nash
Robert S. Pelcyger
Thomas L. Smithson
A. John Wabaunsee
Charles F. Wilkinson

Assistant to the Director
Joan C. Lieberman

Native American Rights Fund

1506 Broadway • Boulder, Colorado 80302 • (303) 447-8760

Of Counsel
Charles H. Lohah
Thomas N. Tureen

Washington Office
1712 N Street, N.W.
Washington, D.C. 20036
(202) 785-4166

Staff Attorney
John D. Ross III

"Brother, the Great Spirit made us all."

Red Jacket, Seneca 1792

Do you agree with Red Jacket's words? If so, I hope you will want to support the Native American Rights Fund.

Why should you help us?

Our aim is to provide fellow Indians with their legal rights according to existing laws and treaties. These include the right to live in self-governing tribal communities, to worship according to our own beliefs, and

- A stated position — by a physician

Dear Concerned Citizen:

I am writing you as a physician.

For you can help the Rheuma/Arthritis Fund end forever the pain, deformities and anguish of arthritis.

As you read these words, rheumatoid arthritis is wrecking the lives and health of one in every eight Americans.

Yet we are told there is NO cure!

Patients are offered aspirin and other pain-killers to alleviate the symptoms. Ruined joints are often surgically replaced.

As a doctor, I don't find stainless steel and plastic implants. Nor do I approve of massive doses of

- A situation described — about the environment

America is in trouble, and
we need your help now.

I'm writing this emergency letter because I know you
understand better than most the work we must do immediately to
protect America's wildlife and environment.

Here's the hazardous situation we face as you read this ...

Right now, in Washington, the financial under-
pinnings from those federal programs which help
insure clean water, clean air, and the
responsible plans that maintain and protect the
environment have been cut. These laws and
regulations which guard our country's natural
beauty and health are seriously weakened, or
are being eliminated entirely.

It's as if they had decided to turn the clock back by
decades to those times when little interest was given to wildlife
and ecology. But, even then, the Federation was calling out for
change and reform.

- And another situation

I withdrew some money our
children need to buy you
the enclosed Christmas cards.
Please, as you use them, think
of these despairing children and
help us care for them.

Death is NOT a nice Christmas present

for a little child . . .

. . . and that is why I am writing you this letter and asking you to support
the Sullivan Children's Home.

For even as children you know are eagerly unwrapping skates, sleds,
bikes, doll houses, and costly video games on Christmas morning, many boys
and girls in Central America would be overjoyed with a thin slice of bread
and a glass of milk.

War, disease, poverty and starvation are especially cruel to children.
Children of dead parents cannot run away, or find jobs, or even beg for food
if adults drive them off.

We have been working for 37 years to save the lives of boys and girls
in many improverished lands.

As you may have noticed, several of these examples don't begin with the traditional "Dear. . ." salutation. They just begin.

This technique, called a "running lead," brings your reader directly into your story, case history, or problem. If you have a good story, this is often more effective than a traditional, less direct opening. Running leads have been criticized on the ground that a letter *must* open with "Dear Something." The answer to this criticism is that running leads have been tested and found to produce improved results when compared with impersonal "Dear Friend" openings.

A running lead is a substitute for the salutation — a substitute that moves directly into the body of the letter. Obviously, it is impersonal. On the other hand, you are not reminding your reader of this by rubbing his or her nose in it via "Dear Unknown." Sometime you should consider using a *personalized* running lead, simply to get your reader right into the main thrust of your letter: "Has it occurred to you, Mrs. Jones, that . . ."

A step beyond the regular running lead is the running lead that begins on the mailing envelope. Usually it's a short phrase that commands attention: "What if armed men took your child away at night, and . . ."; or "The tinkling of a breaking window pane. . . ."

Citizens Committee for the
Right to Keep and Bear Arms

Liberty Park • 12500 N.E. Tenth Place, Bellevue, Washington 98005

The tinkling of a breaking window pane. . .

". . .The right of the people to keep and bear Arms, shall not be infringed."

Citizens Committee for the Right to Keep and Bear Arms

Liberty Park   12500 N.E. Tenth Place   Bellevue, WA 98005   (206) 454-4911

"... the right of the people to keep and bear Arms, shall not be infringed."

The tinkling of a breaking window pane. . .

awakens you. You sense that someone is in your home. Dimly, you recall a newspaper piece about armed burglars who have killed several victims in the Hawthorne area recently.

Frightened, you reach for the revolver in your bedside table. Your fingers search frantically. It isn't there! You remember the gun confiscation law. You turned in your revolver, received a receipt. What good is that piece of paper now.

Footsteps creak towards your bedroom door. You grab the phone to summon help and find it silent... the wires cut.

You hear the handle of your bedroom door begin to turn. Your heart pumps madly. You scream in terror!

    This incident is based on fact. Unarmed, honest people like
you are being robbed, tortured, raped and killed daily.

    That's the best reason of all for you to join the CITIZENS
COMMITTEE FOR THE RIGHT TO KEEP AND BEAR ARMS.

    When a dangerous intruder enters your home, a gun does make
the difference between living and dying.

HOW TO EXPLAIN WHY YOU ARE WRITING

All communications — fund-raising letters included — should have a specific purpose. Your job is to recognize your purpose and then to explain it clearly and convincingly. You should probably do this early in the letter.

Some would-be writers fumble about with the purpose of their letter. They are self conscious at the thought of asking a stranger to contribute. This attitude comes through in the text, and it can cost thousands — maybe millions — in gift dollars. So begin writing by defining a clear, logical purpose for doing so — a purpose of which you can be proud! All fund-raising has a purpose, an important reason that has caused the creation of a mail campaign. Whether your purpose is the saving of lives, providing a quality education, protecting children from abuse, repairing or constructing essential facilities, protecting America from tyranny, restoring a sound ecology, feeding the hungry — this purpose must be an important, visible part of your message. Furthermore, it is the best technique of all to explain why you are writing to total strangers and asking them for contributions.

The next example does an excellent job of explaining its purpose by quoting scientists on the need for immediate action. The writer might have said to himself or herself, "The purpose of this letter is to raise money we can use to rescue the Chesapeake Bay. Here is an environmental disaster in the making — one that can be avoided only by action that requires funding now."

Chesapeake Bay Foundation

Dear Friend of the Bay,

     "BAY IS DYING, SCIENTISTS WARN."

   Sound unbelievable?

   Perhaps, but this headline appeared recently in the Baltimore Evening Sun.

   New facts about the Bay have been developed by top independent scientists in the course of a 6-year research study of the Chesapeake Bay funded by the Environmental Protection Agency. This research shows the Bay is in worse shape than many people believed.

   Scientists working on the study are now speaking out about the damaged condition of the Bay and the need for immediate action to save it.

   We can't allow this to happen.

   We must stop the destruction of the Bay. Our health, our economy, the many pleasures and food we derive from the Bay are at stake.

   That's why I'm writing to you today. To ask you to help Save the Bay by becoming a member of the Chesapeake Bay Foundation.

This letter to donors gives the reason for writing in its first paragraph.

July 16, 19

Mr. & Mrs. L. T. Harley
P.O. Box 6
Williamsburg, VA 2310

Dear Mr. & Mrs. Harley:

        Will you help me get the facts on government funding of left-wing groups out to the American people?

        Thanks to your financial support we at TCCRAEF have been able to dig through literally thousands of pages of government grant documents to uncover Federal funding of left-wing groups and individuals.

Early in a letter, within the first few paragraphs as a general rule, the writer should ask for financial support. By letting the recipients of a fund-raising letter understand its fund-raising purpose, nothing is hidden. And don't be afraid to do it with emotion. In fund-raising by letter, the more emotion that can be conveyed, the better. So, whenever it's appropriate, let an emotional note come through in your statement of purpose. It can only help.

"Unless I can get you to help me now, Andy and other little boys are sure to die."

"With your support, we can begin striving to stop acid rain from killing fawns, and baby rabbits. . . ."

"You're not apt to see blind children. They're not riding bikes down your street, or playing catch in a neighbor's yard. These boys and girls who will never run and play desperately need your help now."

HOW TO MAKE IT BELIEVABLE

Believability is critical to successful fund-raising. When the only reward is the sense of a good deed well done, people who cannot *believe* in that good deed will not give to it. This is a cynical age. Many prospects, especially those who reside in upper income areas, receive a large volume of fund-raising mail and discard the majority. Why? Often because they simply cannot believe in the cause the letter represents or the facts it states. Being a believer, whether in a religious faith or any other cause, is based as much on emotion as on physical evidence, so your letter should provide both. There are several ways.

Facts. Relate an appeal to accepted facts and sources that can — and often should — be quoted. You become believable when your writing is specific. Talking about abused children in the abstract is not nearly as convincing as focusing on a few individual cases and explaining there are 13,042 of these taking place "even while you read these words." It's one thing for the medical profession to claim that smoking can be deadly. It is quite another when a doctor writes: "Not many people realize how deadly cigarette smoke is. Yet this year alone it will kill more than 300,000 of us . . . six times as many as died in all the years of fighting in Vietnam." Or, consider this appeal.

> Many senators facing re-election won by razor-thin margins in the last election. <u>They will have no presidential coattails this time</u>. Nine of these senators have 0% voting records on the key issues I've described.
>
> Slick public relations cannot hide the facts -- 15.2% of our population has slipped into poverty -- <u>21.1% of all children now live in poverty</u>. You and I know, as professionals, that the so-called recovery is a myth. There's more want, more real need, than in many years.

Cautious claims.   Do not exaggerate to the point of being ridiculous. Overkill is not a good idea. It arouses suspicion, which begins with your message and spreads to include your organization. When Chicken Little screams that "the sky is falling," he is so obviously mistaken that nobody pays attention. Unsubstantiated claims made by otherwise sincere groups can have the same effect. Granted, people who are pre-sold on your program — whether it's to eliminate handguns, cure cancer, or whatever — may take everything you say at face value. However, you may be turning off many less convinced individuals. These are people who would also agree with the case you make, if it were proved with documented facts instead of wild claims.

Don't write fund-raising letters for causes in which you cannot believe yourself. They won't be good letters, and they are apt to stray from the truth. On the other hand, if the real facts convince *you,* you can probably use them to convince others.

Illustrations.   Use specific illustrations, including case histories, whenever practical. One problem with case histories is that they must be real. If you invent one out of whole cloth, where do you turn when a potential donor wants to aid a specific victim or asks to meet him or her? Saying "I made it up," isn't going to do much for your credibility. On the other hand, unless you disguise your real case with a false name, you could be subject to a law suit involving invasion of privacy. So when case histories are employed, be sure to use a fictitious name or obtain legally solid written permission from the person whose case is discussed. Even if you just use a photo, you need what is known as a "model release," in which the subject agrees to your using this photo in your fund-raising efforts.

Explain. Do not assume that your prospect has too much knowledge on arcane subjects. Just because your organization is deeply involved in some enterprise does not mean the general public understands it. When in doubt, explain in detail. Jacques Cousteau has done a good job of raising funds on the concept that the seas are becoming overfished and polluted. Yet most of us have never been afloat upon the ocean, or if we were, never saw cause for an environmental alarm. The success of Capt. Cousteau's fundraising efforts results from his ability to explain problems that most of us have never considered or never knew existed.

To explain problems — problems as complex as the environmental aspects of our oceans — you must do two things. 1) You must *yourself* understand the problem in all its complexity. You must yourself recognize the real reason your cause is raising money and see it as a logical, legitimate response to either a major problem, or a major opportunity, or both. Then, 2) you must be able to boil down all that understanding and feeling into a text that even the less involved prospect can easily understand and share. Here, in a couple of paragraphs, is how one writer does it.

```
concern every thoughtful person in the world today.

     You know, as we do, that the pace of destruction
of the ocean and its creatures MUST be slowed -- that
there is, in fact, very little time left.

     I am certain you share our belief that the only way
to achieve this is to rouse the people -- the slumbering
people.  Only they, aroused and armed with the truth,
can turn the tide.

     I give my life to this task.  I ask you to con-
tinue your support by renewing your membership today.
```

Tie-ins. Tie your appeal to something most people already accept, even if you are going to refute it later. Examples of this technique are found in mailings pro and con on the subject of firearms. Hunters and shooters already know that "anti-gunners" want to take away their shotguns, rifles, and pistols. Those who would tighten up on firearm laws are already convinced that the "Gun Lobby" is spending millions of dollars to influence Congress. The same opportunity exists in every emotional or political situation.

"Apartheid is evil." "Congress will bankrupt the country." "Criminals are being coddled." "AIDS will kill you." "Communists are the aggressors."

Congressman McDonald's death gave the Conservative Caucus Foundation a strong "peg" onto which to tie its appeal for funds.

Here's another tie-in. The parallel treatment of human murderers and the death of an alley cat, and the injustice of it all, are exposed for prospects to consider. (The reader tends to come down heavily in favor of the cat.) This is another example of the endless opportunities that lie all around us waiting to be discovered. No matter how prosaic your cause seems to be, there is always an exciting tie-in somewhere. It is your job to dig it out and use the facts in the most profitable way.

```
Dear Human Friend:

      Many people object when a murderer faces execution.

      Yet millions of harmless, lovable pets are cruelly
being put to death this year -- and no one notices!

      Their only offense is that they have no home!

      Yet playful cats and cheerful dogs are needed by many
lonely elderly people and by families whose children long
for an affectionate, playful friend.

      That is why I am inviting you to join the wonderful
group which supports the li...
```

HOW TO ASK FOR THE MONEY

A fund-raiser is basically a salesperson. He or she must "qualify" prospects (determine that they are indeed valid prospects), contact them, convince them that they will benefit by making a contribution, and then "close" the fund-raising solicitation by asking for and receiving a check.

Asking.   One of the prime principles of sales is that orders just don't appear, they must be asked for. Another is that a salesperson must state a price. These principles also apply to fund-raising by mail. Autos, television sets, steaks, spaghetti, and pajamas all have their prices. Your organization must have a price too. It has been proven by many tests over a long period of years that asking for money becomes more effective when specific amounts are suggested. Here's how one group does it.

Why begin by asking for at least $15? The answer is that smaller contributions, especially those of $1 and $5, hardly pay for the expense involved in obtaining them. Even more significant is that, generally speaking, people who send relatively tiny amounts are very difficult to upgrade into giving $15 or more. There are many reasons for this. Some elderly folks have never adjusted their thinking to inflation and believe that $1 to $5 is a very generous gift. Others really are not interested in your organization and donate $5 just so you will go away. Groups that mail low-cost premiums such as address labels with their appeals generally receive a flood of low-dollar gifts from those who feel that they must send something in return for the premium. But because they are annoyed by the necessity of doing so, they will mail only a minimum sum.

Some fund-raisers prefer to start with a maximum suggestion and then scale downward: "Please send $50, $25, $15, or whatever you can spare at this time." They feel that this gift suggestion results in a larger proportion of $50 and $25 checks. That is how it's done in this next example, a telegram-type mailing. (Yellow paper and a telegram format do convey urgency.) The amounts asked for are variables based upon a previous gift.

NA~ ~~~
~~~~ ~~~~~~ ~~~
~~ ~~ ~~~ ROAD
~R~ ~~~~, ~~. ~

MESSAGE SENT TO: Jean Marte~ ~.

MESSAGE SENT: APRIL 25, 19

THE WORST OF MY FEARS HAVE BEEN REALIZED. YOUR HELP IS
URGENTLY NEEDED.

I JUST WROTE TO YOU ON MARCH 25 ABOUT THE NEED TO SET
UP AN EMERGENCY FUND FOR THE MULTI-UNION LAWSUIT.

AT THAT TIME I SAID I DIDN'T KNOW WHAT MIGHT HAPPEN OR
WHEN.

JUST 6 DAYS LATER, ON MARCH 31, JUDGE CHARL~~ ~~~~

I CHECKED THE RESPONSE TO MY LETTER OF MARCH 25. I WAS
SHOCKED. APPARENTLY, MOST OF OUR SUPPORTERS DIDN'T UNDER-
STAND JUST HOW SERIOUS THE SITUATION WAS.

I HAVEN'T HAD TIME TO UPDATE THE RECORDS SO IF YOU
ARE ONE OF THE FEW WHO SENT A CHECK, THANK YOU.

BUT IF YOU DIDN"T RESPOND TO MY EMERGENCY FUND APPEAL,
PLEASE SEND A GENEROUS CHECK NOW.

THIS SITUATION IS SO DESPERATE I HOPE YOU WILL BE ABLE
TO SEND $75.00 BUT IF YOU CAN'T PLEASE SEND $50.00 OR EVEN
$25.00 TODAY.

TIME IS VERY SHORT. I'VE GOT TO KNOW IF I CAN COUNT
ON YOU BY MAY 16 AT THE VERY LATEST.

I WILL BE WAITING TO HEAR FROM YOU.

ANXIOUSLY,

~~O~~~ ~.
CHAIRMAN

P.S. EVEN IF YOU DID JUST SEND A CHECK I HOPE YOU WILL
CONSIDER SENDING ANOTHER. THINGS ARE REALLY THAT BAD.

Specific amount.   The argument is sometimes made that asking for a contribution of unspecified size ("as much as you can afford") may result in some unexpectedly large gifts. In actual practice, it usually brings in minimum gifts. Here's why. Most of us want to discharge our obligations at the least possible cost. On the other hand, assuming you have convinced a prospect to write a check, he or she will probably want to donate an "average" amount. In a sense, this is like tipping at a restaurant. The customer knows that 15 to 20 percent is expected, and usually leaves about that amount. Thus one can avoid being considered either a "cheapskate" or an "ostentatious tipper." That is why many fund-raisers find that defining the size of an expected "average gift" raises additional dollars.

Here is the crucial paragraph from a letter on behalf of the Washington (D.C.) Hospital Center's Needy Sick Fund. It asks for specific amounts yet indicates that any gift, regardless of size, is welcome.

```
critically, ill and injured when they need them most — the instant
they enter the door.  Obviously, many people treated in MedSTAR will
incur costs requiring NEEDY SICK FUND assistance.

     This emphasizes all the more the basic purpose of the Fund - to
pay for treatment that makes the difference between life and death for
someone's beloved.  I feel this is reason enough to write and urge you
to join all of us who are sending $100, $50, $25, $10, or whatever can
be spared.  Please send something.  Your gift, large or small, truly
matters.

     Please make your check payable to the NEEDY SICK FUND.  I'll be
watching my mail for your reply.

                                          Sincerely,
```

Need.   Generally it makes sense to suggest a specific amount towards the conclusion of the letter. By then, the reader understands why you are writing, why funds are needed, what they will be used for, and why his or her gift is essential at this time. By asking for a specific amount and if possible tying it to the costs of a specific need — a school book, a meal, a foot of water pipe, summer camp for a day — a concrete case is made for a gift of a specific size. Here, for example, a political fund-raiser shows exactly what your gift can do for his candidate's campaign.

Until this money is received, a campaign staff cannot be assembled, telephones cannot be installed, literature cannot be printed.

Your contribution of $600 will pay a month's rent for his campaign head-quarters; $325 will pay a week's salary and fringes for a secretary; $150 will buy a used desk; $75 will pay the postage for 340 mailings; and $50 will pay for 340 campaign folders.

Please, ACT NOW to restore fiscal "common sense" to government! Your contribution, today, can help elect a dynamic leader who cares about the American taxpayer.

Sincerely,

Bill

Recognition. Let's examine another way to suggest a specific gift. It has to do with donor recognition. "For a $100 contribution, your name will be engraved in everlasting bronze." "Your $50 gift entitles you to a 14-karat gold-plated membership pin." "Your $25 gift insures we will inscribe your name upon a brick here in the new Memorial Chapel where thousands of visitors will view it today, tomorrow, and forever."

Not only does the following letter offer a different kind of reward, but it also shows that a premium need not be tangible to be effective. Here, a Christian boys' home offers to recognize your donation with the gift of prayer.

We are going to begin preparations for our Christmas celebration here at ....' Home very soon. I'm afraid it just won't be much of a Christmas unless friends like you help. But we'll do the best we can.

And one part of our Christmas tradition that I know we'll celebrate is our Novena in honor of the Nativity of the Christ-Child--December 17th through December 25th. I hope you'll let us pray for your special intentions. It is our spiritual gift to you.

There just aren't many friends like you I can turn to at a time like this.

I know how much you care...I'm just praying you'll find a way to help.

Upgrade. When soliciting past donors, relate your request to their most recent or largest gift. This is what most fund-raisers do when upgrading donors to a higher level of giving. With computer letters, as you'll see in paragraphs five and six of the next example, this is easy.

The Children's Hospital
A Regional Pediatric Health Care Center

November 12, 19

Mr. John . Ca.. .e
Ep~i ~ Data . age.
 New Eng. nd Exe utive
Burlington, Massach etts 018

Dear Mr. .am, 'e:

It could happen at any moment...day or night. A child is rushed into Children's emergency department.

The child could be a young boy who's been badly burned over 90% of his body. Or a girl with internal injuries from an auto accident. Or a baby losing his battle against a life-threatening fever.

Yes, it could be almost anything. And it could end in tragedy unless that child receives the very best in health care...immediately.

It's for emergencies like these that Children's equips its renowned medical staff with the most up-to-date equipment available. Equipment like the 8-channel monitor which quickly measures a child's 8 most vital functions, and makes split second diagnosis and treatment possible.

Equipment like this is expensive. Yet, it is essential. And thanks to generous support like your $10 Memorial gift in January, Children's is able to meet the incredible costs of quality child care and save young lives.

Because your past support has made such a difference, I'm asking you today if you can find it in your heart to send a gift of $15, $25, or possibly more. We will put your dollars to work now saving young lives.

Sincerely,

If you are using inexpensive offset printing (which makes computer personalization impossible), you can still ask for three specific gift sizes using dollar amounts: average, larger than average, and very large, all based on your giving records. This technique becomes more effective if you can segment your donors by giving range — that is, those who've made $10-$20 gifts, those who have made $21-$30 gifts, etc. Then you can design separate printed letters for each segment — being assured of asking for an increase that's not out of the question.

When dealing with small contributors, such as $10 donors, many fund-raisers will ask for a 50 percent increase. Generally as the level of the donor's past giving rises, the computer is programmed to ask for a sum that represents a smaller and smaller percentage of increase. (If very large gifts are suggested, prospects are often encouraged to pledge monthly amounts.) For example, you might have a scale of gifts something like this.

Gifts of $5 or less . . . . ask for $10
Gifts of $10 . . . . ask for $15
Gifts of $25 to $40 . . . . ask for $50
Gifts of $41 to $50 . . . . ask for $60
Gifts of $51 to $60 . . . . ask for $75
Gifts of $61 to $90 . . . . ask for $100

THE RIGHT WAY TO CLOSE

Every salesperson knows that once he or she has a signed order, it is time to head for the door. Otherwise, the customer may raise questions that might negate the sale. And the same in fund-raising: Having asked for a specific contribution, you must assume it will be forthcoming and make a speedy farewell. But how?

There are many ways to close a letter. Consider restating the theme used in opening the letter. Thank the reader, in advance, for a generous gift. Assume that the prospect has decided to give, and assure him or her that the decision was a wise one: "Your gift will enable us to . . ." Or offer personal benefits, as a gospel minister does here.

I urge you to pray for your friend -- then back up your prayers with a gift.

In return, I'll send you the same booklet that goes out to new Christians so you can see for yourself how the Word of God Hour is helping the saved and unsaved alike.

But, take action right this minute, as God leads you. Sit down and write your check, then complete the ballot, and mail them both in the enclosed reply envelope.

You'll be helping me stay on the air.

And maybe even making it possible for your loved one to find the Lord.

This next letter, used by The American Hiking Society, translates the annual membership-dues gift into a tiny, monthly amount. It reminds the prospect of the benefits to be gained by giving, and it asks for immediate action, "today."

Joining the American Hiking Society will cost you $15 annual dues. That's the equivalent of $1.25 monthly. You surely can afford it. And consider the alternative... continued erosion and wreckage of your right to get outdoors and walk.

You'll be proud of your membership card and decal... they'll help you made wonderful new friends along the trail... you'll use your newsletter to discover new hiking places.

What are you waiting for? If you enjoy the outdoors, and hiking, or cross-country skiing, you belong with us in The American Hiking Society.

Do something for yourself, and for nature too... by joining us as a member today.

JK:aa

Sincerely,

James A. Kern
President

P.S. I'm looking forward to welcoming you as a member. We intend to open a Washington, D.C. office where we can work even more effectively for your rights in the outdoors. I hope you'll come see me!

Some groups add a statement about the tax deduction to the end of their letter — a good place for it. There is no real advantage in stressing the tax-deductibility of a contribution throughout a fund-raising letter. The amounts suggested in direct-mail appeals are usually too small to make much difference in anyone's taxes. But more important than the actual deduction is the de facto sign it provides that your organization is recognized by the government as a legitimate, worthy, nonprofit group. This adds credibility to your appeal for funds. It implies that the government has investigated and approved of your organization and its purpose.

delivery of dental care. The Fund has made substantial contributions in these areas.

These are just a few of the reasons for supporting the American Fund for Dental Health.

I ask you to join me in making an investment in our profession. Send a tax-deductible check so the Fund can continue and enhance its vitally important work.

Sincerely,

Frank P. Bowyer, D.D.S.
President
American Dental Association

As for those final closing words, "Sincerely," "Cordially yours," and the like, try to make them continue the general tone of the letter. Some clergy sign off with "Yours in Christ," "In His name," or a similar phrase, which reinforces the idea that this fund-raising letter is a request from the pulpit.

Maybe they have a good idea. Many religious mailings raise huge sums. So it might be worth considering whether the closing words, instead of being conventional platitudes, should relate directly to the appeal. If "Yours for humanity," "Yours for good government," or "Yours for better health," bring in even a single additional contribution, they surely are worth the slight extra effort spent in creating them. After all, ink, paper, printing and postage cost the same regardless of whether your closing is effective or not.

HOW TO PICK THE SIGNER

Generally speaking, the board chairman, executive officer, or a trustee signs fund-raising letters. Sometimes it is possible to use a celebrity signer whose name adds status, authenticity, or appeal to your letter. Ronald Reagan's name appeared upon many appeals for Republican causes because they considered him their most effective fund-raiser. In years past, the signatures of John Wayne, Barry Goldwater, Hubert Humphrey and George McGovern proved highly effective. When Norman Lear, a well-known television producer, signed fund-raising letters for his alma mater, Emerson College, his appeal to fellow alumni succeeded dramatically.

The Wolf Trap Foundation runs a cultural enterprise in Virginia. It picked a great Southern name, Robert E. Lee, to sign its membership mailing. The letter was immensely successful, even though today's residents of the area are largely immigrants from other regions. Robert E. Lee IV, who operates a distillery, is a great-grandson of the famed Confederate general.

While fewer and fewer citizens actually remember the presidency of Franklin Delano Roosevelt, his name has meant a great deal to the Democratic Party. It should, for he transformed it from a minority to a position of dominance through his enormous appeal to fellow Americans. The name of his son, F.D.R. Jr., signed to a letter, turned out to have significance, especially among an older, and presumably richer, generation. The sons and daughters of your cause's great past leaders may also be effective signers for today's letters.

There are pros and cons concerning the use of a well known signature. The plus factors are obvious: name recognition and ego satisfaction at being addressed as an equal by some famous individual, especially when he, or she, is asking you for a personal favor. On the negative side, a name that has been overused instantly lets prospects infer they are reading a ''mass mailing'' instead of a personal message.

Guidelines.   What makes one person's signature more effective in raising money than someone else's? Here are some guidelines.

- *Title or position* — For example, a physician signing a health-related appeal, especially on his or her own office letterhead, will usually come through as an informed authority who should be heard.

- *Personal involvement* — When someone is willing to tell his or her own story and sign it, the effect can be dramatic. If that person has a famous name, so much the better. Whether the signer is a statesman, a refugee, a former hospital patient, a disease victim, or a rescued child, the signature of a first-hand witness — someone who has been on the scene — adds to authenticity and makes the appeal more believable: "You don't know me, but I spent three years at Dachau...."

- *Community figure* — In a local campaign, a minister, mayor, city manager, prominent athlete, or other local leader may be more effective than someone directly connected with the project.

- *Noted personality* — A letter from a famous person will usually get opened. Bear in mind though that the vast majority of successful fund-raising letters are not signed by noted personalities. To be most effective, a famous signer should have a convincing letter to sign, a logical relationship to your cause, and a reason for involvement, as Ms. Hepburn's with Planned Parenthood.

Katharine Hepburn

Dear Friend,

Normally, I don't get involved in public controversy. But reproductive freedom is a basic, <u>personal</u> issue, and one that I feel very strongly about for personal reasons.

Over 50 years ago, my mother helped Margaret Sanger found a new, controversial organization called the American Birth Control League. That organization later became Planned Parenthood, and since then has been in the forefront of providing family planning services to millions of Americans.

Now, I have joined Planned Parenthood in carrying on my mother's struggle so many years later because there are two proposals that will be considered by the next Congress that could destroy completely all of her tireless work.

Planned Parenthood has never lost sight of Margaret Sanger's and my mother's original goal: to give all people the right and the ability to determine for themselves whether and when to bear children.

These brave women knew even then that no woman, black or white, rich or poor, can ever truly be free without the right to personal control over her own reproductive life.

You now have an unique opportunity to become part of this historic debate. Neither you nor I should expect "someone else" to take our responsibility. Everyone's help is desperately needed.

Please send as much as you can today.

Sincerely,

Katharine Hepburn
for Planned Parenthood

Finding a signer. Here is a final consideration: How do you go about enlisting a suitable signer? The question may never arise. Your letter may be signed by your organization's president, board chairman, or some other officer, or by the director of development.

Yet some letters, especially those mailed throughout the nation, may call for better-known, more distinguished, or more notable signers. If that's the case, your first question should be whether getting someone special to sign your letter is worth the effort. If the answer is "yes," the next step is to make a list of possible signers, and to contact as many as possible. The easy way to contact a celebrity — an actor, entertainer, musician, etc. — is through a board member or someone else who knows your potential signer on a personal basis. For example, if you are raising money for a symphony orchestra, your conductor may be on a friendly footing with some well-known musicians. If this is out of the question, you may need to approach an agency that represents celebrities. In the United States, these agencies usually are located in New York City or Los Angeles. If you need assistance, check with a local advertising agency, especially one that handles advertisements involving endorsements. They can generally help.

With politicians, it is even easier. You can write them at their offices, and follow up, if need be, with a telephone call.

Well-known individuals usually face a barrage of requests for their names and their support. When you write to them, you should explain why their signature is important, what it will help you accomplish, and how it will enable them to help accomplish something worthwhile. And another consideration: Everyone wants to be seen as a fine and generous person. (Adolf Hitler made a big show out of being kind to little children.) Personalities in politics and the entertainment world benefit from having good press, and an association with your organization might help them achieve that goal. So, stress the benefits to the signer as well as those to your cause.

Naturally, you will never want to use anyone's signature, photo, or identity without having their permission to do so on file in writing. Without such permission you and your organization are possible targets for lawsuits.

Bear in mind that the effectiveness of any signature depends on its believability. It could be better to have an unknown local physician sign your letter than a famous thoracic surgeon, if that surgeon obviously cannot be very familiar with your local hospital. All other things being equal, the closer your signer's association with your cause, the better. If you decide to use a signer whose association with the cause is not clear, then add a paragraph or two to explain — perhaps in the signer's own words — why he or she is an appropriate signer.

WAYS TO MAKE YOUR P.S. PAY OFF

The postscript is an extremely well-read part of the fund-raising letter. Originally, the P.S. was a device that conveyed a thought the letter-writer had overlooked earlier. Then studies showed that a person will often read the P.S. before he or she reads the body of the letter. With that discovery, writers started reserving the P.S. position for their strongest points.

So your letter should probably have a P.S. — one that's well thought out. There are several effective ways of creating postscripts.

- *Personalization* — With a computer-generated letter, using the addressee's name or town in the P.S. is an easy and natural way to strengthen an already strong text, as Mr. Burke may have discovered when he received this political appeal.

I sincerely understand if it is impossible for you to contribute this much at this time. However, if you can-not, please write me and let me know. Our budget has been carefully planned in the hope that everyone could contribute again, and we would like to know if we will have to organize an emergency alternate plan.

Sincerely,

Dick Da

Dick Da 1

DD/ml

P.S. The Los Angeles Times just released a poll showing that Max is trailing Alan Cranston. If Max is to win, Mr. Burke, he will need your support more than ever.

- *Restate your case* — Many effective postscripts sum up the fund-raising appeal in a few brief words. If you assume that people will read your P.S. before they read your letter, an interesting summary in the P.S. may lead to a careful study of your full letter. This P.S. by the Good Shepherd Lutheran Home of the West sums up the short, one-page letter in a single sentence.

for whatever you can send and wish you the most joyous Christmas and a blessed New Year.

With gratitude,

F. D. Geske

F. D. Geske
Executive Director

FDG/lt

P.S. Your tax-deductible gift of $15, $25, or more will help us serve those of God's people who are mentally retarded and win souls for Christ.

Serving the mentally retarded since 1956

- *Consider ''handwriting''* — A short, printed reproduction of handwriting, matching that of the signature and perhaps in blue ink, adds emphasis and makes the letter appear more personal. Here, Mr. Westhoven uses two postscripts, one typed and one written.

Sincerely,

Rev. Tom Westhoven

(Rev.) Tom Westhoven

P.S.   Remember -- you can't buy these Indian
         originals in <u>any</u> store. They're uniquely
         <u>yours</u> to send -- as a one-of-a-kind way
         to show that you care.

P.P.S. AND REMEMBER, TOO, IT ONLY TAKES $120
TO HELP PAY FOR A CHILD'S ENTIRE YEAR
HERE AT ST. JOSEPH'S. AND EVEN $15
GOES SUCH A LONG WAY! ALL GIFTS ARE
FULLY TAX-DEDUCTIBLE, OF COURSE!
THANKS AGAIN.   T. W.

St. Joseph's Indian School   Chamberlain, S.D. 57325

- *Rephrase the request* — The P.S. is a good place to restate the need for a contribution, saying it differently and perhaps adding another good reason not included in the body of the letter. In this example, the appeal is rewritten negatively and effectively.

In Christ,

H. Balthasar Lawrence

H. Balthasar Lawrence

HBL/uv

P.S. Please remember, when you don't vote in favor of
     the Word of God Hour, you are casting a vote
     by default -- in favor of the forces of evil.
     But I know you are on God's side. So I urge you
     to send back your ballot immediately!

- *Ask for non-gift help* — For example, asking the prospect to "get a friend to help," is often an effective way to involve a person who has not yet decided to give. Action on Smoking and Health uses that approach here.

          Please use the enclosed envelope to mail ASH your tax-deductible
contribution for $100, $50, $25, $10, or whatever you can. By helping ASH,
you'll breathe easier. We all will. The lives saved by ASH may well
include our own dear friends and loved ones.

                    Sincerely yours,

                    Alton Ochsner

                    Alton Ochsner, M.D.

P.S. If you can't help ASH now, please write and let me know. I'd appre-
     ciate it if you would suggest a friend who can help. All contributors
     receive the ASH Newsletter which keeps them up to date on the vital
     issue of smoking and health.

- *Special reasons* — When nothing else is available, the postscript provides an opportunity to state a very special reason why a gift is needed at this moment. You can usually come up with some special reason. Look at the reason used by Greenpeace USA, in its fight against the seal-hunting business.

```
                  moment, right now, to send us your check.
Send whatever you can, $20, $30, $50 or even $100, but
please do it now.  Spring is nearly here and the slaughter
is about to begin.  Again...


                              Thank you,


                              Douglas Falkner
                              Administrative Director
                              GREENPEACE International

P.S.   This year is a critical year for the seals.  We are
       expanding our efforts to meet the challenge, but we
       need your help.  In fact, in the month before the EEC
       decision we spent over $100,000 on a European
       advertising campaign to put pressure on the EEC
       nations to implement an import ban.  This costly ad
       campaign, as you can see, was effective but has
       seriously hampered our cash flow.  Won't you consider
       an increase in the size of your donation so we can
       continue to meet the challenge?
```

Of course, none of these techniques needs be used alone. Consider combining two or more. But watch out for redundant, meaningless, or confusing postscripts. Remember that the postscript should probably be the most carefully designed element of any solid gold fund-raising letter.

Writing an excellent letter is not enough. Unless properly "packaged" it may not fulfill its potential; it may not even reach your prospect. But what is packaging?

So far, all we have talked about are a letter and a mailing list. You will need more than that. You'll need an envelope in which to mail the letter, an address on the envelope, and postage, too. These essentials will get your letter to your prospect. But what if your "solid gold" text works as planned and the prospect wants to make a gift? Then you need a form for the prospect to fill out — a form telling who is making the gift, how much it is, and what it's for. Finally, you would be well advised to provide a self-addressed envelope in which the prospect can return the gift.

These packaging elements — mailing envelope, address, postage, gift form, and gift envelope — along with your letter, are sufficient to raise money. But with a few extra elements you may be able to raise even more! Usually, these additional packaging elements are what they call "inserts" a folder, a photo, a premium, another letter, or a questionnaire. This chapter will look in detail at all these basic and additional packaging elements.

MAILING ENVELOPES THAT INCREASE GIFTS

Your mailing envelope (or "outgoing" envelope) has two jobs. First it must deliver the appeal to the prospect, and then it must induce the prospect to open it. This second job is critical. Effective fundraising by mail depends in large measure on whether or not the mailing envelope commands enough attention and interest to be opened.

In the United States, the basic mailing envelope is probably a white #10, or possibly #9, window envelope. (A #10 envelope is the standard business size; #9 is slightly smaller.) The window is used primarily because it insures against any possible mismatch of name and address — Mr. Black's personalized letter going into Mr. Green's personalized envelope. Another reason for the window envelope is that it looks businesslike and therefore "deserves" to be opened.

5 FRI

For many years it was more or less sacred writ that no headline or message should appear on the outgoing envelope of a fund-raising mailing. Such "envelope slugs" as they are termed were supposed to smack of commercialism and hurt response. Then some fund-raisers tested printing messages upon the envelope. In some cases they found such slugs increased gift response, especially when raising funds for highly emotional issues. To anyone who lives in Maryland or Tidewater, Virginia, for example, this envelope carries a significant message — one that makes opening the envelope a logical next step.

If a fund-raising mailing envelope looks important, it is likely to be opened. This one tells you by its very appearance that it's important.

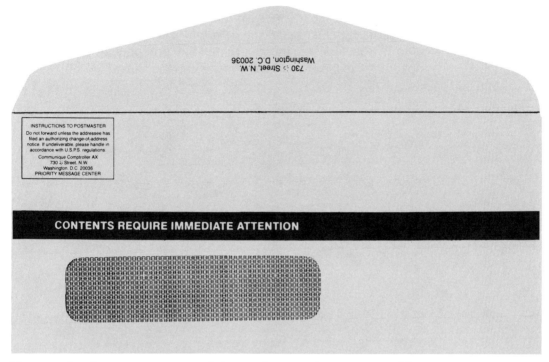

You can begin your message right on the envelope, even with a photo. Here is a photo of a U.S. Senator. IndependentAction once used this envelope to raise funds in hopes of defeating him at the polls.

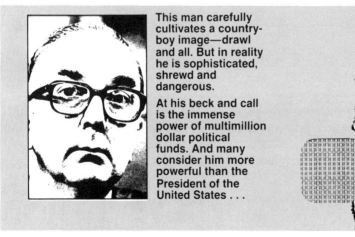

This man carefully cultivates a country-boy image—drawl and all. But in reality he is sophisticated, shrewd and dangerous.

At his beck and call is the immense power of multimillion dollar political funds. And many consider him more powerful than the President of the United States . . .

In the next example, the non-controversial but official-looking delivery instructions and the text about a "legal judgment" virtually assure that the prospect opens this envelope from the Citizens Committee for the Right to Keep and Bear Arms. But strong envelope headlines like these mean the fund-raiser must back them up. It's not enough just to get the envelope opened. Unless your message inside justifies the headline, the prospect is likely to feel tricked and to toss the whole mailing into the trash.

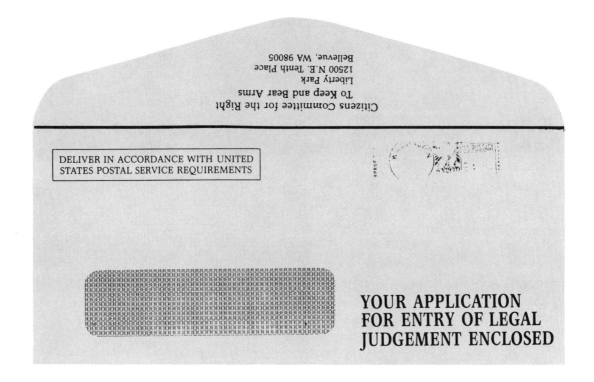

This envelope slug always seems to work well in tests. If you're using expensive postage, don't hide the fact; print it on the front of the envelope.

Of course, there are many ways to capture a prospect's interest, and one of them is just to look interesting and appealing. Who could ignore this letter from Chris?

The color of an envelope can affect whether or not it's opened. Market research indicates that brown kraft envelopes tend to be opened; envelopes made from brightly colored stock tend to be opened less. Most fund-raisers play it safe with white envelopes and perhaps some printing in colored ink.

Consider using a real, pasted-on stamp rather than printed or metered postage. Here are some pros and cons. The cheapest way to mail is by printing the postal indicia on the envelope; there's virtually no additional cost. The next cheapest method is to have your mail metered — that is, run it through a postal meter, which most mailing houses can do for you. Affixing a real stamp, whether by hand or by machine, will generally cost more than metering.

What is the difference in results? Will one method make your appeal letter bring in a higher net income than the others? There are tests that indicate a pasted-on stamp can heighten response — especially if the rest of your envelope's components, and particularly the way it's addressed, make it look like a personal letter and if the material inside continues that impression. Along the same lines, if it looks like a personal business letter, then you can probably get the similar heighten response by using metered postage. But the final answer is the standard one you hear in direct mail: test. Used convincingly, first-class postage and paste-on stamps generally will bring in the most response. The real question is whether they will produce *enough* extra response to pay for their cost and to increase the net profit. This is a question worth asking, especially if you are mailing in huge quantities. Then even a tiny increase in the percentage of response can make huge differences in your gift income. Each cause, each mailing, is unique. So test.

In summary: The mailing envelope must deliver the letter to your prospect. It must induce him or her to open it and to be receptive to the contents. In addition, the envelope should accurately reflect the message and the circumstances of the message inside.

HOW TO DESIGN A GIFT FORM

The gift form is the part of the mailing package on which the prospect tells you that he or she has decided to make a gift (enclosed, or coming later). In direct-mail sales, it is called an order form, or reply form, or response device.

Early fund-raisers often printed the gift form on the letter. Most early computer letters did the same. They were designed to be returned to the sender as a unit, together with the contribution. That made it difficult to mismatch names and addresses on the letter and gift form. And it made sure you would know your donor's name and address — regardless of their handwriting. It also saved the costs of printing a separate gift form. However, testing has since indicated that a separate form may improve results to a degree that more than compensates for the additional costs of paper, printing, and correlation.

Some fund-raising groups continue to combine both the letter and reply form on a single sheet of paper — apparently with good enough results. Their fund-raising mailings usually seek to reach a huge number of potential donors at minimum cost. The gifts of those who respond are eventually upgraded by more conventional — and expensive — mailings.

Gift forms may take a wide variety of formats, but all try to make certain that the name and address of a donor and the essential direct-mail coding are included when the gift comes back. If you place this information on the form yourself — via computer or a label — it will guarantee that you have it in a legible condition when the form is returned. (As a variation, some groups affix the address label to the rear of the gift envelope, which is then inserted in the mailing envelope so the label shows through the window.)

Incentive and involvement offers described in your letter, and a brief summary of your basic appeal, should be restated on the gift form. The prospect will almost certainly be looking at the gift form when he or she makes the truly final decision about how much to give: the moment at which the check is written. This is a crucial time at which to remind the prospect of the key points of your appeal.

Another powerful ingredient for a gift form is imagination. In the next example, the gift form takes the shape of a memorandum from the donor to the President of the United States, something that few nonprofit causes can attempt. But any cause can direct a similar memo to someone who is impressive enough to command attention. This example nicely restates the basic points of the appeal letter. Then it guides the prospective donor into beginning his or her response — starting with a box that doesn't even represent a monetary commitment, then moving to a box that represents only a commitment of unspecified amount, and finally to a box that promises a gift of specific size. This involvement technique is a skillful and gracious way to shape the final moments of decision.

Memorandum to:

President of the United States

     I want you to know I support the new direction
you are leading our nation. And I want to see us
continue the way we are going towards full economic
recovery.

     I recognize the growth of federal spending is
slowing down, inflation is nearly under control, and
federal regulation is being reduced. I believe
that's good for every American.

☐   I pledge to support Republicans who will work to
support your efforts to restore our nation to
the greatness and prosperity we once had.

☐   Further, I am enclosing my contribution to help
you contact voters all over the country and give
financial aid directly to Republican congres-
sional candidates.

     My check is made payable to the 19   Victory
Fund in the amount of:

☐ $_____ ☐ $100   ☐ $50   ☐ $25   ☐ $15
    other

     I want to do all I can to help you win this
election so we don't return to the disastrous
policies of the past that nearly led us to
economic collapse.

Sincerely,

_____

Mr. & Mrs. .tt :⸱ ⸱
PO Box ⸱⸱
Williamsburg, Virginia 23⸱'

More examples follow on the next two pages. The first is a variation of the memo-to-the-President technique. The form presents the prospect with an easy sequence of boxes to fill in: first, you agree with the cause's stand; second, you say that you have mailed a post card to help cause; and third, you say you will make a gift. This gift form uses the format of a memo. The first side of the memo is computer-typed, personalized and localized. And the message is continued, in printed form, on the rear of the memo.

The second gift-form example on the next pages reminds prospects of a powerful case history described in the appeal letter. It asks for the contribution, and then it goes on to involve the prospect further with a "non-detachable" survey in which the donor is asked for information that will further help the cause. The survey form has a "return by..." deadline — something that would be difficult to add to a gift form alone. Psychologically, it may not be easy for a prospect to send back the survey information while leaving the gift form blank.

MEMO

FROM:
         Program Director

TO: Jean Mar
         Box
         Williamsburg, VA 231

The issues to be discussed at CITES are, indeed,
complex and numerous.

Yet endangered species are especially important to
all of us because we have a real responsibility to
protect this unique wildlife for future generations.

Even in the Commonwealth of Virginia a number of
species are endangered which are threatened by
killing, capture, and trade, including:

* Finback Whale
* Sperm Whale
* Loggerhead Sea Turtle
* Bald Eagle

(over, please)

**ENDANGERED
SPECIES
PROJECT**
Action Reply Form

I agree that endangered species, such as the Minke Whale, Green Sea Turtle, Gray Wolf, Hooded Seal, Grizzly Bear and over 100 other unique species must not be pushed into extinction because of the inaction of the United States and other foreign governments.

I have mailed my postcard to Secretary of State ⸱⸱⸱⸱⸱⸱⸱⸱⸱⸱⸱⸱⸱⸱ and asked him to strengthen U.S. resolve to push for strong conservation measures at the CITES meeting to be held in Africa April 19-30.

I am enclosing my tax-deductible donation to help ⸱⸱⸱⸱ continue to work for strong U.S. and international policies protecting endangered species.

Contributions are tax-deductible to the extent allowed by law.

( )$40   ( )$25   ( )$15   ( )$ Other

Jean Mar   013513
Box 6
Williamsburg, VA 231

Please make checks payable to ⸱⸱⸱⸱ and mail to:
⸱⸱⸱⸱⸱⸱⸱⸱⸱⸱⸱⸱⸱⸱⸱⸱⸱⸱⸱⸱⸱⸱⸱⸱⸱⸱ **th Street,** ⸱⸱⸱⸱⸱⸱⸱⸱⸱⸱⸱⸱⸱⸱⸱⸱⸱⸱ 0⸱0

To: ██████, Chairman

 The abuse of workers like ███████████ must be stopped. I'm enclosing my maximum contribution to help fight the ███████ bosses and make them pay.

☐ $15   ☐ $25   ☐ Other $_____

From: Jean Mart█ s
       █rten██ █ █a█
       Post Office Box 2
       Willia █urg, Va   2310█

To be removed by Foundation personnel only.

Survey

 The problem of union corruption and violence is growing every day. But the Foundation's ability to fight compulsory unionism abuse is also increasing, thanks to your support. Your response on this CONFIDENTIAL survey will help us target the areas where the most union violence and corruption is occurring, so we can concentrate our efforts in these areas.

 Please answer the questions below. If you have any further comments on this subject, please use the back of this sheet.

 Thank you.

Return By July 5th

1) Your age group: 21-39 ____   40-55 ____   56-65 ____   over 65 ____

2) Are or were you a union member?   Yes ____   No ____

3) Are or were you covered by a voluntary or mandatory pension fund?

   voluntary ____   mandatory ____   none ____

4) If yes, do you think the highly-publicized corruption in union pension funds is present in your city?

   _____

5) Have you or a member of your family or neighborhood ever been subjected to violence, harassment or loss of your job because of union boss abuse?   Yes ____   No ____

Comments: _____

_____

_____

Your initials please: [   ]

Offering a membership, this organization designs its gift form as a business reply card. It invites the prospect (among other options) to check the "yes" box and to be billed later. Attached to the form is a premium — an Interim Membership card that allows the prospect to begin enjoying membership benefits immediately. On the back of the Interim Membership card, are listed all of the benefits of membership — a repeat of information contained in the mailing's cover letter. At the bottom of the gift form, new members are told what part of their annual dues represents a tax deductible gift.

INTERIM MEMBERSHIP

The bearer of this registered card is an Interim Member of the Na·ic·al······ and is entitled to all privileges of membership including free admission to Na···al ···· historic properties for this interim period.

Member

2/15/8.

Valid for 30 days from the date shown above.

№ 183

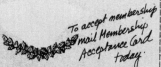

To accept membership mail Membership Acceptance Card today.

Membership is being held for you under this registered number for the next 30 days. Retain the card above for identification until your validated registration arrives.

№ 183

☐ **YES,** I accept the invitation of the President. Please validate my Membership and start sending all of my membership benefits, including ······· ······· magazine. I understand I do not need to send money now. I will be billed for the annual dues of $15 later.

MRS. JEAN MAR·
BOX (
WILLIAMSBRG, VA   231(

Please make sure your name and address are shown exactly as you wish them to appear on the Na······ ···roster.

☐ To simplify paperwork, I enclose my check for $15 in advance.

☐ I believe the work of the ·············· warrants a special contribution. My check is made out for $_____ more than the cost of membership.

Of the total amount of your dues or contribution, $3.00 is for a subscription to *Preservation News*, and $6.60 is for a subscription to ············· for one year.

BUSINESS REPLY CARD

FIRST CLASS   PERMIT NO.)2   ···IN·· ·

POSTAGE WILL BE PAID BY ADDRESSEE

·····················
········ ··········· Avenue
··············)C).

NO POSTAGE
NECESSARY
IF MAILED
IN THE
UNITED STATES

Membership Benefits and Privileges

- ··············· magazine
- ·········· *News*
- Free admission to ····· historic properties
- Tours, exhibitions, workshops
- Discounts on books & gifts
- Annual conference

And most important, the knowledge that you are helping to safeguard America's cultural and historic heritage.

If you are already a member of the ············ or have received more than one mailing, please excuse the duplication. We appreciate your support of preservation and hope you will pass this on to a friend or colleague who might be interested in joining the ·····.

And here's a cause that seeks a regular monthly gift, — one made through an automatic bank transfer that's authorized once by the donor but valid until the donor cancels the authorization. A monthly pledge makes the gift look small, but an innocent-looking $5 per month is an annual gift of $60. This kind of gift form is somewhat more difficult for the donor to fill out than the others shown here. But the "perpetual" type of gift that can result from a bank transfer arrangement could easily offset any reduction of the response rate created by the more difficult form. Notice that the basic appeal about "puppies, kittens, dogs and cats" is reinforced again on the gift form — just when it counts the most.

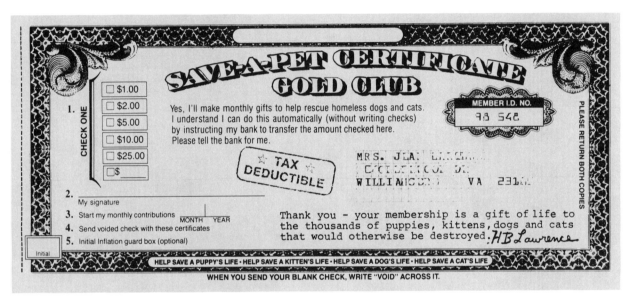

On the next page, the NRA Institute sends prospects two attached gift forms, each with a different deadline. The idea is to generate two separate gifts from each donor, spaced a few weeks apart. To strengthen the two-gift idea graphically, the decorative border of the first form is printed in blue ink and the border of the second form is printed in red.

MEMO from the Executive Director NRA INSTITUTE FOR LEGISLATIVE ACTION

Dear A. L. Cone, Jr.,

As Executive Director of the NRA Institute for
Legislative Action I want to personally assure you
that the entire ILA staff has geared up to do whatever it takes to defeat this precedent-setting
legislation proposed in California and all other
gun laws.

To win it's going to take every NRA member to
do literally more than his share. Please consider
the critical situation we're in and send the largest contribution you can afford today. Thank you.

J. Warren Cassidy
Executive Director

AUG. 7th DEADLINE

REPLY MEMO

TO: Harlon B. Carter

FROM:

A. L. Cone, Jr.
Box 4
Williamsbur., VA 231

JMB3501D
3B

☐ YES, I'm sending my maximum contribution to help the NRA Institute beat this
grave and senseless new nationwide threat to our gun rights.

☐ $25.00   ☐ $50.00   ☐ $75.00   ☐ Other $ _____

☐ NO, I cannot help the NRA Institute at this time.

Make checks payable to: NRA Institute for Legislative Action, P.O. Box 1730, Washington, D.C. 20013

AUG. 30th DEADLINE

REPLY MEMO

TO: Harlon B. Carter

FROM:

A. L. Cone, Jr.
Box 4
Williamsbur., VA 231

JMB3501D
3B1

☐ YES, I'm sending my maximum contribution to help the NRA Institute beat this
grave and senseless new nationwide threat to our gun rights.

☐ $25.00   ☐ $50.00   ☐ $75.00   ☐ Other $ _____

☐ NO, I cannot help the NRA Institute at this time.

Make checks payable to: NRA Institute for Legislative Action, P.O. Box 1730, Washington, D.C. 20013

Any gift form, of course, should take its tone from the appeal letter and from the cause itself. This appeal from a religious cause invites the prospect to add a note about a "divine healing." The prospect is encouraged to fill in and return the divine healing part of the form and to pledge a gift just below it.

Brother ⬚⬚⬚⬚⬚, believe with me for a divine healing for --

_____

_____

_____

_____

_____

_____

_____

_____

_____

_____

_____
Name

A.L. Cone, Jr.
P.O. Box .
Williams⬚ ⬚g, VA ⬚ ⬚

Brother ⬚⬚⬚⬚⬚, I'm planting
this seed to help you take
God's healing power to this
generation.

☐ $10
☐ $20

☐ YES! Send my alabaster box.   ☐ $_____

Keep this portion of my prayer sheet as a point of contact.

PARTNER,
    LET GOD SPEAK TO YOU
    ABOUT "YOUR DEPTH" OF
    COMMITMENT AND THE
    SEED YOU SHOULD PLANT
    THIS MONTH IN THIS
    EXPANDING, WORLD-WIDE
    MINISTRY.   B.L.

In the next example, a cause dedicated to lobbying for a citizen's legal right to bear arms has designed its gift form to resemble a legal document. But the document turns out to be a questionnaire that guides the prospect into a clear recognition of the need to make a contribution that will defend his or her constitutional rights.

Notice the information telling the donor how to make the check payable and giving the full mailing address of the cause. Even when you enclose a self-addressed gift envelope, it's absolutely necessary to show your cause's complete mailing address on the gift form, just in case it gets separated from the rest of the mailing. The gift form should contain all the information the prospect needs to decide to make a gift and send it to you.

Application For Entry Of
Legal Judgement

1
2
3
4   Citizens Committee For The Right
    To Keep And Bear Arms
5   _____
    Plaintiff
6
7   **Extra**
                                                     Civil
8   United States of America   **Action**
    _____
9   Defendant
10
11
12 On reading and examining the decision handed down by the U.S. District Court in
    Morton Grove, Illinois,

13 **It Is Ordered, Adjudged And Decreed** that I feel the Second Amendment of
    the U.S. Constitution protects and guarantees the right of every American to keep and
14 bear,

15 ☐ rifles   ☐ shotguns   ☐ handguns
    ☐ none of the above   ☐ all of the above
16

It Is Expressly Decreed that the "militia" referred to in the Second Amendment refers to the

☐ **American people**   ☐ **National Guard**

It Is Further Adjudged that the gun rights guaranteed to every American by the U.S. Constitution cannot be taken away by states and cities.

☐ **Yes**   ☐ **No**

It Is Finally Ordered that the Morton Grove law banning possession of a handgun is

☐ **unconstitutional** ☐ **constitutional**

And Whereas the cost to protect and defend the constitutional gun rights of every American is the responsibility of every concerned gun owner, I am enclosing my check in the amount of:

☐ **$15**   ☐ **$25**   ☐ **$50**   ☐ **$100**   ☐ **$**_____**other**

to help fund the massive legal and lobby efforts being waged by the Citizens Committee For The Right To Keep and Bear Arms to overturn the Morton Grove decision and stop the spread of similarly inspired laws in states and cities across America.

Signature _____

Name _____

Address _____

City, State, Zip _____ Phone: (_____)_____

Please make your generous check payable and mail this Judgement Form to The Citizens Committee For The Right To Keep and Bear Arms, Liberty Park, 12500 N.E. Tenth Place, Bellevue, Washington 98005

Now let's review those elements that *must* be included on any gift form.

- *Name and address of donor* — There is no point in receiving an anonymous contribution. Because, if you do, you may have a gift, but you have no donor to contact in the future — nobody to renew and upgrade. Therefore, you need a name and address for your files. The donor is usually given space in which to write this information. But so many people have poor penmanship or forget to fill in the blanks that most fund-raisers design the mailing so that the address label is on the gift form. This insures that the address is accurate (because it was delivered) and readable. An alternative is to place an address label on the rear of a gift envelope, but this means that you may lose those who use their own envelope to reply.

- *Size of gift* — We have already discussed the need to suggest gifts of specific sizes within the letter. This should be repeated on the gift form. It stops vacillation on the donor's part. Checking the box next to a specified amount, and sending a check in that sum is quick and easy. The donor needn't invent his or her own amount, which may be too small by your standards.

- *Purpose of gift* — When your letter ties a gift directly to some specific use (like buying a sack of rice or a bale of used clothing, or providing a scholarship for some worthy student) this purpose should be repeated on the gift form. Whether it's $13.55 for 20 dozen eggs, or $15,000 for a piece of scientific equipment, the donor wants his or her gift to satisfy the intended need.

- *Summation of basic appeal* — Whether you're raising funds to ban the bomb, save the porpoise, stop drunken driving, or accomplish any other goal — your basic appeal should be summarized on the gift form so the donor is reminded of the reason for giving, reminded at the moment of truth when he or she begins to write the check. By the time this happens, your appeal letter may be lost or in the trash, having served only to get your gift form into the prospect's check-to-be-written pile. If your letter gets you this far, it has done its job well; but you need another reinforcement of your appeal at the instant before the check is written — a vivid reminder of why the gift form was placed in the checks-to-be-written pile.

Because of this, you should get it in your mind that the gift form is an intrinsic part of writing the appeal letter; they are virtually the same thing.

- *Involvement device* — Not every letter or mailing package needs a survey, post card, questionnaire, or other involvement device. But if you use one, it's wise to tie the involvement device tightly to the gift form — if not physically, then in words. Even if the involvement device resembles a petition or note to a congressman, which must be physically separate, it should be at least mentioned on the reply form.

- *Immediacy* — If your prospect feels he or she can postpone the decision about a gift, your contribution will never arrive. The need for action NOW must be emphasized on the gift form to overcome inertia.

- *Code* — How can you tell which of your efforts is producing the most income unless you can attribute individual responses to specific mailing packages and lists? Every mailing you make should be a learning experience for you. A code on the gift form (perhaps on the mailing label) will help you identify the mailing from which the gift resulted and let you find out what is working, what isn't, and what you should consider doing next. Mailings are expensive and such codes (usually called a "key code" or a "key number") help you pinpoint which of your many list and mailing-package options may be the most profitable. You can't test without them.

- *The basics* — Finally, there is some basic information that *absolutely must* be included on every gift form. Here it goes. 1) The complete, correct name of your organization. 2) How to fill out the check. 3) Where to send the check: a complete mailing address. 4) To what degree the gift is tax deductible. And 5), any other legal disclosures or advice that must be given if the donor is to be ethically well informed in making a contribution. All this information may have appeared elsewhere in your mailing package. But remember, at the moment just before the check is written, the only part of that package that you can assume remains in the prospect's hands is the gift form. So it must be designed to do the whole job.

TIPS ON GIFT ENVELOPES

The purpose of the gift envelope (or the "reply" envelope, or "business reply envelope" as it's called in the direct-mail trade) is clear enough; it's to carry the gift form and the check back to the cause. One specification of the gift envelope is also quite clear: It must be small enough to fit within the mailing envelope. It must also be large enough to hold the gift form and the check, and it would be best if it held them without the necessity of folding them. (Many people seem to dislike folding things to insert them into an envelope.)

After these self-evident truths, opinions about the gift envelope become a bit less firm.

What about postage? Can the gift form be a part of the gift envelope? What color paper? How large? What text? And do you really even need a gift envelope?

We will answer each of these questions. First, let's answer the last one. Yes, you need a gift envelope if you want to receive a gift. If you ask people to use their own envelope and to address it themselves, you may find that some will not bother, and your response rate will drop.

If you just want the pledge of a gift, you could consider printing your gift form on the back of a business reply card that needs no envelope. But that's another bad idea. Many people don't want information about their charitable gifts — or intentions — to be visible to the general public. They may cringe at the idea of making a pledge on what's basically a post card. So, even when only seeking pledges, it's best to send a gift envelope.

The rest of the questions can be answered quickly. There are no cut-and-dried answers; everything varies too much from cause to cause, from mailing package to mailing package. The only way you can tell what is best for you concerning postage, colors, size, etc. is to — you've probably guessed it — *test.* Test one form of, say, postage against another. The results will give you an answer that applies to your case. But let us look at each of the questions anyway and see what your options are.

Postage.   Because the objective of most gift envelopes is to increase response by providing convenience, many fund-raisers have included postage in the form of either an affixed stamp or a business reply permit printed on the gift envelope. With postal costs increasing, the trend at this point may be towards letting those who respond provide their own stamps. Naturally, this probably will not increase response. If anything, it may decrease it. On the other hand, many tests have demonstrated that an organization's savings on postage more than compensate for any lost contributions. There is no hard-and-fast rule, so test. Something to think about is that any business reply envelope must have a ''commercial'' appearance, while a plain addressed envelope, with or without stamp, may seem somewhat less commercial — more ''needy.''

Real postage stamps glued to a gift envelope may increase response. The problem is their high cost. After all, they are mailed to everyone, including those canny individuals who will soak them off to use on their personal correspondence. Therefore, affixing postage works best when used with limited lists of previous large-gift donors to whom you are mailing auto-typed or similar highly personalized letters and from whom a high response rate can be expected. When the response rate gets high enough, a real stamp actually costs less than business reply postage.

Some mailers have even experimented with ''multiple'' stamps. For example, they might apply four five-cent stamps and several one-cent stamps to the gift envelope. They feel that this array tends to attract attention and to discourage soaking off the stamps.

If you're going to provide a stamp for the gift envelope, you may find it most effective to attach that stamp lightly to the letter rather than to the reply envelope. This then *involves* the donor in gluing the stamp to the gift envelope — an activity that can increase response. Here is a political appeal using this technique. Notice though how the loosely-attached stamp isn't just left for the prospect to discover; the letter focuses attention on it — personalized attention — at the beginning and the end, the two strongest positions in a letter.

CONSERVATIVES FOR CARTER
FOR SENATOR

BOX 5. • & J. P. WHITE BUILDING
ROSWELL • NEW MEXICO • 8820
TELEPHONE (505) 265-_9

Robert C. Ha.~yc~, *Chairman*   Kenneth ~u~, *Vice Chairman*   Robert ~. ~~, *Treasurer*

Please use this stamp
and let me hear from you
today, Mr. _inley.

October 3, 19

Mr. ~rn~ 'inley
~0~ . Ocean Drive
Fort Lauderdale, Florida 333_

Dear Mr. _inley:

I wouldn't write you again unless it was urgent. I just don't
know what else I can do. I simply must ask if you can spare another
$10.00 to make sure ~~~ Carter defeats Joe Mo~ c~a.

Only the last critical weeks of the campaign are left,
Mr. _inley. ~~~ Carter has come up very fast and we are only about
4% behind in the polls with 12% of the voters uncommitted. But
we've run out of money. This means no more newspaper ads, no more

tnis man to remain in the U.S. Senate, Mr. inley, and I don't
think you want him there either.

In haste,

Robert G. Ha~ g

Robert G. Ha~ g~~
Chairman

P.S. Please use the enclosed stamp today, Mr. inley, and give all
you can to help ~~~ beat Joe Mo~ ~a. The need is critical. Please
let me hear from you at once.

Size, color, etc. Here are some more thoughts. Small gift envelopes tend to get lost in the mail. The larger the reply envelope, the less likely it is to be overlooked, either by your prospects or by the postal service. On the other hand, larger envelopes sometimes — but not always — are more expensive.

What about the gift envelope's color? Does it really make any difference? A white envelope printed with black ink is the traditional choice. But when in doubt, test. If color coordination is significant, perhaps with a sweepstakes or other special graphic design, both colored paper and colored ink may merit consideration.

A gift envelope can also serve a double purpose. There are ''wallet-style'' envelopes that double as the gift envelope and gift form. This means you don't need a separate gift form; an extra-long envelope flap provides space for that. The only problem is that space on a wallet-style envelope is limited, and there often is not enough room for anything more than listing a few suggested gift sizes. On the other hand, though, such an envelope saves the printing and stuffing costs that come with a separate gift form and also allows room for a message on the outside of the flap.

Here is an example of a simple wallet-style envelope. On the front there is the address of the cause. The outside of the long flap is used for a summary of the appeal in the form of a quotation by someone important to the cause. On the rear of the envelope — covered by the flap when the envelope is sealed — there is a small but sufficient gift form. (If necessary, this cause could also have used the additional printing space available on the inside of the flap. Remember though, there is glue at the end of the flap of a wallet envelope. Don't position fill-in spaces in the glue area; what's written there will be obliterated. If you write anything at the very bottom of the envelope, where the flap attaches, it also will be obliterated. Many causes print a design of some kind at the bottom of the envelope and at the bottom of the flap to discourage the prospect from writing in those spaces.)

"The quality of American life is so dependent on the creation of children by choice rather than by chance. The program of Planned Parenthood-World Population is deeply concerned about the population problem from the point of view of what it contributes to the quality of life, particularly to the strength of the individual family — not only to the parents, but to the children yet unborn."

Dr. Alan F. Guttmacher*

Former President
Planned Parenthood Federation of America

• Deceased March 18, 1974

PENINSULA PLANNED PARENTHOOD, INC.

1520 Aberdeen Road

Hampton, Virginia 23666

Outside of envelope and flap

ANY contribution entitles you to membership in

Peninsula Planned Parenthood, Inc.

Sponsor	$100.00	Friend	$10.00 ....
Patron	$500.00	Student	$ 5.00 ....
Contributor	$25.00		

Name ....

Address ....:.....   Zip Code ....

Contributions are deductible for income tax purposes. Please make checks payable to Peninsula Planned Parenthood, Inc.

Thank You For Supplying The Postage

Rear of envelope

WILL ADDITIONAL INSERTS RAISE MORE?

Anything that can be mailed can be used as an "insert." All you do is insert it with your letter. Here are a few examples: booklets, post cards, surveys, opinion polls, sweepstakes coupons, key chains, pads of labels, reproductions of newspaper and magazine articles, photographs, reproductions of invoices and memos, question-and-answer folders, additional small letters or notes (possibly associated with a case history), financial statements, repair estimates, thermometers, tea bags, flower seeds, bumper stickers, descriptions of special premiums, etc.

Whenever you are creating a direct-mail package for fund-raising, ask yourself if an additional insert might strengthen response? If your cause isn't well known, the reprint of a positive newspaper article describing your work might convince prospects that you are worthy of a gift. If there is just too much information to put into a reasonable-looking appeal letter, an additional data sheet — maybe in a question-and-answer format — will help prospects make a decision in your favor. Inserts are usually not the most expensive part of the mailing. The right one can pay for itself quickly and produce a profit. The most important criteria for inserts are that they must be a functional part of the mailing package, accomplish a specific purpose, and reinforce your primary message (not divert attention from it). This means that annual reports and treasurer's statements generally are not helpful (unless they add to the validity of an emergency appeal). Test several inserts against each other; test your package with and without an insert. Keep in mind the first rule of inserts, which might be stated as: "Never use an insert without an excellent reason." What are some reasons? Any insert must accomplish one or more of the following.

- Reinforce the message of the letter by adding believability. These days, many potential prospects worry that their money will either be wasted, or is requested for an nonessential cause. Reproductions of newspaper clippings, or invoices, or estimates, or handwritten appeals from needy individuals, or similar documents can help to increase the believability of your appeal.

- Reinforce your emotional appeal. Assuming your appeal letter is emotional, a folder may reinforce the emotion with facts. It can also anticipate and answer questions. Because fund-raising appeals sometimes create suspicion, it never hurts to prove the honesty, integrity and usefulness of your organization and its accomplishments and goals.

- Give the prospect a worthwhile task to accomplish. People enjoy small, simple tasks. They want to express their individuality by participating in a cause that supports their own interests or feelings. Surveys, opinion polls and post cards are a proven means of helping such donors to express themselves. (A word of warning! In the United States, post cards or letters addressed to government office holders may be ruled as lobbying and can lead to problems with a cause's nonprofit status.)

- Let the prospect express himself without fear of retribution. Surveys and opinion polls generally are designed to preserve anonymity. They let the prospect blow off steam to a fund-raiser who promises to present the survey results to important officials. As long as officials seem to be swayed by public opinion, surveys and opinion polls will build response.

- Give the prospect a chance to win money or prizes. Sweepstakes offer the opportunity for winning. They also may let the prospect support a cause that he or she would rather not examine too closely. Cancer is a good example. Everyone fears it. Most people won't even willingly read about it. Yet fund-raisers have succeeded in raising cancer research funds through the sweepstakes approach. This unconventional idea provides an opportunity to make a gift (in the guise of trying to win a prize) to those who do not wish to be fully reminded that cancer is a disease that threatens everyone.

- Present a case history. Sometimes, especially when using costly personalization techniques to produce your letter, it is less expensive to present a case history in a printed enclosure than in the letter body. This case history could take the form of a social worker's report, a clergyman's account of some atrocity, a painfully written note from a child or other victim. Or it could be a medical report, or an on-site observation by an eye witness.

- Illustrate a problem. A good picture sometimes accomplishes more than any written words. The impact can be truly shocking. However, too gruesome a picture may tend to hurt response. Those of hideous deformities, heaps of dead fetuses, and the like may produce such a feeling of repulsion that the mailing is thrown away. Strangely, many prospects are most open to providing help to healthy, attractive people — people who are attractive to the prospect. So pick your photo with your prospect in mind, and then test.

- Demonstrate desired results. Plans for a projected hospital wing, an entrance to a park, a church building, lend credence and purpose to an appeal. They explain how the prospect's money will be used, perhaps even show where his or her name will appear on a plaque or other memorial.

- Display premiums or other benefits. If you offer luggage tags, jewelry, plaques, or other gifts in recognition of contributions, show prospects what they can expect to receive.

Now, let's look at a few examples.

Post card.   This post card insert is addressed to the Secretary of State of the United States. The donor is asked to put his or her own postage on the card, to sign it and to mail it. Doing this involves the donor in helping the cause more actively than just by sending a gift of money. Such a sense of involvement and commitment can increase gift response to an appeal. Meanwhile, the Secretary of State's office gets a feel for citizens' opinion.

```
Dear Mr. Secretary,

I want to express to you my deep concern over the
policy positions and the lack of scientific ex-
pertise of the U.S. Delegation to the CITES Conference
scheduled for April 19-30.

The U.S. government must not oppose much needed
protection for whales and seals.  Nor must it support
weakening of trade controls which protect many other
endangered species, including green sea turtles.

Please, for the sake of all endangered wildlife, do
not allow the U.S. Delegation to pursue its
disastrous policies at the CITES Conference.

              Respectfully, _____
```

Another letter.   An effective insert to go with your appeal letter can even take the form of . . . another letter! One example of this is a small extra memo that says, more or less, "Read this ONLY if you do not plan to help." Inside is a personal note from some executive or special person pointing out what you will miss by not acting at this time. The objective is to drive home the salient points one more time. This technique is overused, done to death. But it's sometimes quite effective.

But that's not the only type of letter-with-a-letter enclosure. Here, the fund-raiser for a summer camp enlists a camper named Bobby as the signer of a second-letter enclosure that reinforces the appeal made in the first letter — using a refreshingly different perspective and voice to do so. It's handwritten on yellow, lined note paper.

Dear Mr. Hilns,

I am hoping to come to camp again and you should know that since last summer my school marks are way up, I have a lot of A's and B's now!

I'd like Susie to get to camp too. She's my sister but a good kid who feels that no one likes her or cares what she does. Im scared for her because she hangs around with real bad kids. When I try to get her to do homework and stuff I don't know what to say.

So please let her come to camp with me and find out that cause your poor don't mean nobody cares.

    She needs a chance to
get outdoors and see the
stars and see that everyone
isn't poor like us.

            Your friend,
            Dobby

P.A. If Susie and me can't
    go please let her go
    instead cause I won't
    go then.

Q & A format. The question-and-answer format is an efficient and interesting way to get information across. And by marking the questions clearly, as the Foster Parents Plan has done here, the prospect is allowed to scan quickly through this two-page insert to find the exact questions that have been bothering him or her. While the format is efficient, an 8½″x11″ sheet filled with type can look deadly. So the Plan has wisely broken up the type with attractive pictures of some of the children they are helping.

Questions and Answers about
FOSTER PARENTS PLAN

Becoming a Foster Parent...

Q. What do I gain as a Foster Parent?

A. You participate in helping a needy child and family in a country overseas while learning something about the social and cultural conditons. This is not mass relief work to starving millions — but personal work with individual children, their families and communities. You feel a deep satisfaction as

Q. Is Foster Parents Plan a legal adoption agency?

A. No. The child remains with the family. We try to help strengthen family units, and enable each member to realize his or her full potential. This is the only way to build strong, cohesive communities in the developing nations where we work.

Q. How will you choose a child for me?

A. You may request a boy or girl between the ages of 3 and 14 in any country where we help

Reprints. Reprints of newspaper or magazine articles give your appeal what is called "editorial sanction" — the newspaper or magazine legitimizes or supports your cause with its editorial or its reporting. This can be extremely convincing to prospective donors. Many causes print the newspaper article on a sheet of newsprint, the type of paper used for newspapers. Most identify the newspaper and underline the mention of the cause's name. When using this kind of insert, remember that newspapers and magazines are almost always copyrighted, and you must request written permission from the publisher to reprint the article.

JUL 5 19˚

Freedom, or . . . ?

EDITORIAL

Over in Chamblee, Ga., Mrs. Doris Glover has filed a $1 million damage suit against the Teamsters International and local unions for incidents she claims grew out of her insistence on working during a strike against her employer. A hearing in Fulton County Superior Court is expected soon.

What's behind such a claim? The question of freedom, she says.

Mrs. Glover's suit alleges that during a Teamsters strike, she and other employees who crossed the picket line became victims of violent incidents — many directed against female and older employees. She alleges threats of violence from the picket line leader, complete covering of her car with yellow paint and slashing of the car's tires.

Other employees, she says, reported shots at their homes from firearms, and the burning tified that they were hired for $50 by a Teamsters official at the plant to set the blaze. The publication adds that a Teamsters official and her husband, were convicted in February of this year of conspiracy to commit first-degree arson.

In this civil suit, for damages, burden of proof is, of course, on the plaintiff. No one should assume that the defendants will be found liable until proper and sufficient evidence brings forth a court decision.

Nevertheless, it cannot be denied that if the facts are as alleged, that sort of situation is indicative of a callousness which completely ignores one of the basic freedoms of Americans — the freedom to exercise the pursuit of happiness in the form of remunerative employment.

Two young men, according to *Foundation News Advisory* (publication of the Right to Work Legal Defense Foundation) tes-

Report. There's nothing like a first-hand report from the trenches to convince the prospect that what you're doing is important. On the next page, a person who sees himself as having been wronged writes to a cause whose goal is to prevent such wrongs. The three-page, handwritten letter is reproduced by offset printing, in blue ink on white, correspondence-size paper. It is one thing to hear of such cases from the fund-raiser, but it's a much more powerful experience to hear of them directly from the victim. If you use such a letter, of course, you must first obtain the written permission of the writer. Even though the letter is sent to you, some aspects of legal ownership and a right of privacy are retained by the writer.

Sept 15, 19 .

‗ ‗ ‗ ‗
‗‗‗ Lerri Line
o‗‗ / ‗ao‗‗ Rd
‗‗‗ ‗ ‗ e‗, Virginia, 21‗

Dear Sirs —

Recently, I have learned of your organization
and its work against Compulsory Unionism,
and their abuses.

I have been a paying member of the
‗‗‗‗‗‗‗‗‗‗‗‗‗‗‗‗‗‗‗ union, Local ‗‗
Denver Colorado. They started a strike
July 16, 19 , one in which I was forced to
attend. I stayed out with the union until
Oct 26, 19 . I Returned to work the Same
day, as I Received a letter from the ‗‗‗
‗ ‗‗ Co, asking me to return to work, or
Loose my Job.

A series of harrassements, from the union
President, the secretary, members of the
local union from my department, and other
departments of the Company, began
immediately.

These harassements included, telephone

My problem is getting an organization to
assist me with my Problem. I Trust you will
accept My Views, and will accept My Case.
Your reply will be greatly, appreciated.
Sincerly
‗‗‗‗‗ ‗ ‗ ‗‗ ‗

Premium offer. An offer of a free gift comes in this attractive, four-color insert from the Hour of Power. You are asked to return the gift card or to write to obtain it. This is what they call a "premium" offer in the direct-mail trade. It's in the same ballpark as "free" lapel pins and similar jewelry items that are sent in recognition of a gift. And, while the cost of the premium item may not be high, offering it can often increase response to your appeal and raise your net gift income. But the premium must be appropriate to your constituency, and it must be something prospective donors would like to have.

There are Easter seals, Christmas seals, and finally Seal seals! Prospects are asked to place these premiums on their correspondence to show their support of the Greenpeace effort to "Save the Seals." Doing so is an immediate act of involvement on the part of the prospect, something that often helps boost response to the appeal. When the premium comes with the appeal letter (rather than after the gift), as these Seal seals do, it is called an "up-front" premium.

The Inner Circle, a politically oriented membership organization based on a $1,000 minimum gift, uses an insert to spell out its very attractive benefits for charter members, a type of premium offer.

Inner Circle

·o·· ·n· .ı , Chairman

The Inner Circle is sponsored by the National ·ıⁿuᴄ·ıᴇ· ᴅ·ɔ ᴇ°ᵉᴬᵛ Committee exclusively for contributors of $1,000 to $4,000.

CHARTER MEMBERSHIP BRINGS:

Clear and continued recognition of your position as a Charter Member.

● Your distinctive Inner Circle lapel or collar pin will be unique for Charter Members.
● Your personalized gold Charter Membership card will also be unique. Each card is consecutively numbered within each state, with the first member from each state receiving card number one for his/her state. Your

group face-to-face, give-and-take meetings with ·.··. .ᴬ· ·. Senators.

● Inner Circle luncheons and receptions for members and Senators in cities across America for personal two-way briefings on proposed policies and pending legislation.

On-going contact on matters of importance and matters of just plain fun.

This insert describes premiums that Colonial Williamsburg offers to donors at various giving levels. If you are offering premiums to encourage larger gifts, it's not a bad idea to promote them conspicuously. This insert does that job effectively and in good taste. Notice the use of antique graphic designs.

In Gratitude for Your Support

ALL CONTRIBUTORS OF $25 OR MORE RECEIVE

Our quarterly, *Colonial Williamsburg Today*, containing news, features, and a calendar of events for the capital city of colonial Virginia.

Information about special events at Williamsburg and our seasonal catalog of reproductions and gifts.

A copy of our Annual Report, a retrospective look at the highlights of the past year.

ALL CONTRIBUTORS OF $50 RECEIVE

A copy of the beautiful book, *A Window on Williamsburg*, a full-color, intimate glimpse of restored Williams-

Matching gift check.   This technique, in which you send the prospect a check and ask him or her to match it, is described in Chapter 2.

Invitation.   This insert invites the prospect to listen to a radio program produced by the cause. Doing so will further involve the prospect in the cause's work and can only help increase response to the appeal. Even if the prospect does not tune in, the insert demonstrates that the International Lutheran Laymen's League is doing things in a major and dramatic way toward "bringing Christ to the nations." The same technique can be used to invite the prospect to attend an event.

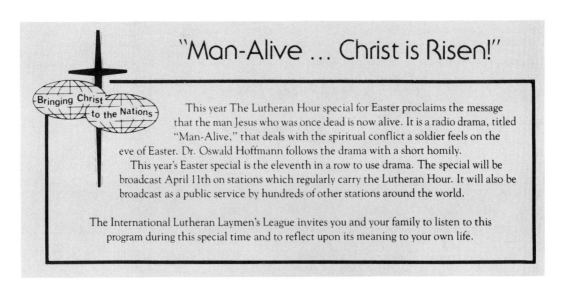

"Man-Alive ... Christ is Risen!"

Bringing Christ to the Nations

This year The Lutheran Hour special for Easter proclaims the message that the man Jesus who was once dead is now alive. It is a radio drama, titled "Man-Alive," that deals with the spiritual conflict a soldier feels on the eve of Easter. Dr. Oswald Hoffmann follows the drama with a short homily.

This year's Easter special is the eleventh in a row to use drama. The special will be broadcast April 11th on stations which regularly carry the Lutheran Hour. It will also be broadcast as a public service by hundreds of other stations around the world.

The International Lutheran Laymen's League invites you and your family to listen to this program during this special time and to reflect upon its meaning to your own life.

Inside peek.   An internal document — an inside peek at the "real" story — is a convincing way to demonstrate the problems your cause is facing. It could be an outstanding bill. It could be an internal memo proposing a project in a way that an appeal letter could not. Or it could be a confidential case report like this one. Its very appearance makes the prospect interested in reading it. It personalizes what could otherwise be a "faceless" appeal. Notice how the names and other identifying information are blacked out — something that only makes the document more interesting, as does the "CONFIDENTIAL" stamp.

CASE REPORT

████████████████████████ *CONFIDENTIAL*

1. Name ____████████████____ _____ Jennifer
                    Family Name   Given Name

2. Date of Birth March 7, 19██ 3. Sex _____ 4. Religion None

5. Place of Birth Dorchester 6. Now living in Foster Home

7. Father Michael ████████ 11. Mother Ann ████████

8. Date of Birth 19██ 12. Date of Birth 19██

9. Place of Birth Boston 13. Place of Birth Arlington
                                             mother's whereabouts

10. Occupation (deceased) 14. Occupation unknown

15. Names of all brothers and sisters, their ages and whereabouts:

Full Name of Brother or Sister	Lives at Home	Does Not Live at Home	Sex	Age	Remarks
Michael, Jr.		Institutional School	M	7	

16. Referral made by: Neighbor concerned for safety of Jennifer

17. Background and General Information: Jennifer's father had been ill for many years
with Multiple Sclerosis. Her mother is a very angry person who often kept Jenny
home from school to be her housekeeper.

This extremely difficult situation rapidly deteriorated after the hospitalization of
Jenny's father due to a stroke which caused him to lapse into a coma.

Jennifer's mother became even more abusive and continually assaulted the child
verbally and physically. Jenny's emotionally disturbed mother blamed Jenny for all
her misfortune.

Because of the family situation her younger brother was her only friend and totally
Jenny's responsibility. Due to the mother's abuse and complete rejection, Jennifer's

The objective of direct-mail fund-raising is to secure, in an ethical way, the highest possible net income up to the maximum actually needed by the cause. These results do not happen accidentally. They are rarely based on luck, although good luck and good timing are always a welcome bonus.

Too often a director of development sits down with pad and pencil, determines how much income the board members will give or get, and then adds in the anticipated results of dinners, foundation appeals, phonothons, media appeals, and other techniques. The remaining difference between that total and the goal is then allocated to direct-mail.

This type of planning overlooks a very significant point. The ability to raise money by direct-mail does not necessarily correlate with your organization's needs. Rather, it hinges on the strength of your philanthropic "case" and on how much work and budget have been invested in developing responsive donor and prospect lists and in creating productive letters and other mailing pieces. If you lack a strong case, good lists and effective writing, your direct mail may produce a minus instead of a plus.

Therefore, your direct-mail goal should be based on hard evidence — proven results that measure your success with case, lists, and writing. And it should be based on available budget, staffing, and time.

With that much said, let's now consider what direct mail can achieve, when it can be used, how much money and how many new donors it will obtain, and what profits can be expected.

PLAN YOUR MAILING PROGRAM

How much money do you need? When will you need it? What is your gift potential? These are sensible questions. Effective direct-mail fund-raising begins with establishing goals, a budget, and a mailing schedule. Will there be a building campaign in February? Are

HOW TO RAISE MAXIMUM DOLLARS

6

Thanksgiving and Easter important to your organization's prospects? Will you be celebrating a special anniversary — perhaps a centennial? What calamities must you prepare for: hunger, disease, starvation, genocide? Questions like these are part of the overall planning effort. Here's another key consideration.

Budget.   There is no point in planning mailings if you cannot afford to buy the envelopes, or pay postage bills. And you must be able to afford to lose much of that budget. To assume that your mailings will result in enough cash to show a profit, or even to pay all of their bills, could be a disastrous error. Your cause must be capable of losing the money it invests in fund-raising by mail and still remaining solvent. You need a secure, *separate* budget that will provide whatever money you require for donor mailings, list testing, copy testing, and other prospect mailings. So the next question you should ask is, "How much can we afford to spend?"

You should also estimate your gift income. If possible, this estimate should be based on previous experience with various mailings for the same cause over a period of years. Best of all, based on tests. But if you are with a new organization, or one that has never used direct-mail in its fund-raising, all you can do is make a rough estimate. Base that estimate on whatever past experience you may have had together with whatever suggestions you may develop from consultants and colleagues involved in similar fund-raising for similar groups. Make your estimate conservatively low.

Once you have a general idea of goals, income potentials, and costs, it is time to sit down with your fiscal officer and work out the financial details. Then, when you understand how much money you will have to spend and when it will be available, you can go ahead and prepare a rough mailing schedule for the next few months, or an entire year.

Schedule.   Bear in mind that your mailing schedule cannot be cast in concrete. You should review it at least monthly in terms of results and costs and fine-tune it accordingly. You may find that mailings must be curtailed or cancelled because the lists you expected to produce large quantities of donors tested out to be disastrous. You may also find that you are raising far more money than expected and should expand your horizons with additional mailings.

Your schedule should be flexible, easy to change, and able to contend with all the variables that influence direct-mail fund-raising results. As Scotland's Robert Burns points out in his poem, "To a Mouse," the best laid plans can come up short of expectations, yours included. Times and results change constantly, and you must always be prepared to change with them — efficiently and happily.

On the next pages you see an example of a schedule, projected for a purely mythical organization in a relatively non-controversial area of work. (You'll note that, to make it easier to follow, this schedule has skipped a few essentials. Specifications should be more detailed than you see here for such things as: preparing envelopes, letterheads, gift forms, enclosures, etc.; reviewing texts; and ordering lists. In addition, the schedule should also include the mailings you'll use to upgrade donors' giving levels.)

ANNUAL FUND RAISING CALENDAR FOR NORTH AMERICAN
CONSERVATION COUNCIL -- 19XX

Mail Date	Project & Materials	Lists & Quantities	Deadline	Estimated Net Income
1/11/XX	New Year appeal to donors	Donors as indicated	12/18/XX	
	Major donors: auto-typed letter; outgoing envelope #10; reply envelope #6-3/4; first-class stamp on outgoing; no other enclosures	$100+ donors: 5,000	" " "	$75,000
	Regular donors: computer letter; outgoing envelope #10 window; reply BRE #6-3/4; metered bulk nonprofit on outgoing; enclosure: memo from Senator Jones	$10/$50 donors: 131,000	" " "	$125,000
2/14/XX	Early Spring prospect mailing: standard "Oceans of Earth" letter; computer addressing 2-page offset letter; #9 outgoing window; #6-3/4 BRE reply	exchange with Widgit Foundation: 25,000 exchange with Whopper Whale League: 30,000	1/20/XX	$10,000
3/17/XX	March-Spring donor mailing new leter	Donors as indicated		
	Major donors: auto typed letter; #10 outgoing envelope; #9 reply envelope; special insert (?)	Major donors 100+: 5,000	2/23/XX	$63,000
	Regular donors: 2-page laser letter; outgoing envelope #9 window; reply envelope #6-3/4 BRE; special insert (?)	$10/$99 donors: 131,000	2/23/XX	$115,000

Mail Date	Project & Materials	Lists & Quantities	Deadline	Estimated Net Income
4/10/XX	Prospect mailings including list tests			
	Copy to be selected from established letters; #9 outgoing window envelope; addressing on reply form; #6-3/4 BRE reply envelope; enclosure to be selected later	exchange with Friends of Water: 10,000	3/2/XX reply forms for outside addressing	$15,000 (with luck)
		exchange with Island Wizzard Walkers: 10,000	3/5/XX remainder	
		50,000 continuation Database Donors, Inc., based on test last year	" " "	
		30,000 continuation with Progress for Passion Forum		
5/10/XX	May donor mailing (special acid rain appeal)	Donors as indicated	4/20/XX	
	Major donors: auto-typed letter; outgoing envelope #10; 1st class stamp; #9 reply envelope; new acid rain letter; enclosure: reprint of news article on acid rain	$100+ donors: 5,300 (with additions)		$55,000
	Regular donors: 2-page offset letter; enclosure: new acid rain letter; older reprinting news articles; #10 window envelope outgoing; address on reply form; #6-3/4 BRE	134,000		$120,000
June	Convention Month – No Mailings Scheduled – Get together with Board Chairman on 6/5/XX to discuss mailings for balance of year. Plan to test copy in July and lists again in August. Hope to continue donor mailings at about 60 day intervals and build donor lists through additional exchanges.			

Mail Date	Project & Materials	Lists & Quantities	Deadline	Estimated Net Income
7/7/XX	Late summer donor—Part I (Part II to be mailed next month as carbon of this mailing)		6/15/XX	
7/14/XX	Prospect tests; list extensions; also copy for fall mailings	133,000 30,000 15,000	6/20/XX	$120,000 $5,000
8/10/XX	"Carbon" mailing to donors	115,000	7/17/XX	$55,000
8/25/XX	Prospect mailing (same lists as April); use alternate control package	120,000	8/4/XX	$70,000
9/18/XX	Fall theme donor mailing; new copy	140,000	9/1/XX	$130,000
10/15/XX	Prospect mailing; use all available proven lists – by exchange and rental	100,000	9/27/XX	$30,000
11/17/XX	Big Thanksgiving appeal – 1st class mail to donors	150,000	10/31/XX	$100,000
12/7/XX	Holiday mailing to all proven prospect lists	120,000	11/15/XX	$50,000
12/21/XX	New Year's mailing to donors – 1st class	150,000	10/31/XX	$100,000

142

RAISE THE DONOR'S GIVING LEVEL

If you have 10,000 donors willing to give $10 each, that equals $100,000. If the same 10,000 donors average $100 each, you'll bring in $1 million. The difference between $100,000 and $1 million is considerable. With about the same mailing costs, you might have $900,000 more income. Not bad!

Agreed, this is all theoretical. But it does illustrate why you should strive to upgrade the gifts of your donors. You may not be able to move all $10 donors to the $100 level, but you'll move some of them to that level, some even higher, and many at least above $10.

The way to get donors to contribute more is to ask them to do so. Use personalization and suggest an upgraded gift. People who are sold on your organization can probably be sold on contributing a larger sum. Sometimes, you need to offer special recognition to secure larger gifts. Educational institutions establish all manner of "President's Councils" and the like. The Colonial Williamsburg Foundation has special meetings — by invitation only — for major donors. They are wined, dined, escorted about historic sites, and made to feel exceedingly important (which of course they are).

But there are many other ways to upgrade your donors' gifts. Here, step by step, is how you go about it.

Initially. Your first move is to try to acquire new donors who make fairly large gifts on the initial request. Generally, the larger the initial gift, the easier it is to get the donor to upgrade his or her giving level the next time around. Some lists and some appeal techniques tend to produce donors whose gifts are difficult to renew or upgrade. Because of this, it is important to keep careful records showing how the new donor was acquired and what his or her performance was afterwards.

Try to keep away from mailings that produce exclusively small donors or donors who are difficult or impossible to upgrade.

Motivation. When you plan your new-donor mailings, design them so you can figure out later what motivated the new donors to make their first gifts. By understanding what motivated people in the first instance, you are better equipped to decide what may entice them to give again and to give more.

Renewal.   Another step should come before you make a serious effort at upgrading a new donor's giving level. That step is the renewal of the gift. Before asking for an increase, you want to make giving a routine, habitual thing in the new donors' lives. You can quietly suggest that it wouldn't hurt if they gave more. (And keep careful track of those who upgrade so easily). But you don't want to make any vigorous thrust toward upgrading until the new donor is safely in the fold and has made at least a second gift. Here is a letter that demonstrates this concept. It spells out the donor's previous gift. It asks for an additional contribution, hinting that an even larger gift might be nice. But there is no direct request for an upgraded gift — not yet.

YMCA
of Greater New York

422 Ninth Avenue, New York, N.Y. 10001
(212) 564-1300

October 9, 19

Mr. John D. amp
sil Data Manage
2 New Engla d Execu e Park
Burlington, Massachusetts 018

Dear Mr. amp :

    I'm writing you today for several important reasons.

    First, I want to thank you personally for supporting your YMCA. Friends like you who sent $10, as you did in 19 ., truly help the YMCA-YWCA Camping Services.

    Your support is again needed. Everything we do costs more than ever before...yet is needed more than it ever was.

Benefits.   Design a benefit program that brings the donor more and more significant recognition as he or she increases in level of giving. Many causes build these programs in a series of easy steps. A $100 gift puts you in the "Century Club," which offers one set of benefits. But if you continue to upgrade your giving to, say, $150, you are then invited to join the "Founders' Associates," for which the giving level begins at $200. As a Founders' Associate, you receive even more attractive recognition. And on up it goes until the natural limit is reached.

All of us enjoy personal recognition. Our name on an honor roll, a certificate for the office wall, an honorary degree, the list goes on and on. Attend just about any performing arts event, and the program will probably feature a list of patrons. You may be sure that some of them gave enough to become a patron largely for the pleasure of seeing their names alongside those of socially prominent patrons. More than one organization has the names of its leading benefactors engraved on the marble walls of its entrance lobby. Other types of recognition include invitations to exclusive gatherings, invitations to attend dress rehearsals of concerts and operas, and so forth.

Recognize longevity.   Generally speaking, few donors stay with an organization over a long peiod of years. They die, retire, move away, or (even worse) lose interest. Many of them simply vanish, and you never discover why. This can be a real loss, because long-term donors tend to be loyal donors — easily responsive to emergency appeals. They're often giving at a generous level because of your upgrading efforts, and they represent excellent prospects for even larger capital or planned gifts.

Careful attention to increasing a donor's motivation to give also may increase that person's longevity as a donor. Your upgrading program, with its increasingly attractive benefits, may help, too. The causes that enjoy the longest donor longevity seem to be those that offer benefits the donor would loath to give up. For example, the arts do well. Those who subscribe to symphony orchestras, operas, or museums, tend to keep subscribing. They attend and they give, year after year. In return for their support, they enjoy clear cultural and social advantages. Academic institutions also do well with alumni, who often are still receiving "old boy" benefits years after they've left college — alumni trips, reunions, networking that's helpful in business, an alumni magazine, admissions preference for their children.

If your cause can offer donors benefits like these, by all means, do so. But if you can't, there's still a technique that helps to build longevity: reminding the donor over and over that his or her longevity is building. If you send personalized letters, it's easy: "For the past seven years you have played an important role in our fight against...." If you don't personalize, you can still group your donors and speak of their longevity, "for more than five years," or "for over a decade." With this technique, each year that passes can bring your donor closer to you.

PICK THE BEST MAILING DATE AND FREQUENCY

You should develop a feel for those events, dates, and special opportunities that can help increase your gift income. Environmental groups seem to mail effectively during the winter months. Drought in Asia may appear even more real during a long hot U.S. summer. Anniversaries, openings, special concerts, memorials, and the like should be considered. Remember that emotional involvement requires a focus. Look for focal points throughout the year and base your mailing schedule upon them. If none exists, create some.

Frequency of mailings sometimes can be a controversial subject. Many boards don't like the thought of approaching donors too often. But what is "too often"? That depends on your group's needs and your donors' responsiveness. Some groups have different frequencies for different donors — based on how each donor is seen to respond best. Few people these days seem offended by quarterly mailings. On the other hand, a monthly approach may be too much unless you can come up with 11 or 12 special — and believable — situations. The answer, of course, is to test for the frequency that produces the most profitable gift results.

SAVE MONEY ON PRODUCTION

There's little point in raising more money if you throw all the new income away on needless production costs.

Bear in mind that while fund-raising counselors have considerable value, it is mainly in the realm of ideas and experience. Use them to spark your thinking and to help with specialized creative tasks. But consider handling the production chores yourself. While it is hard work, supervising the production of your mailings can be very profitable. When you turn this over to an outside firm, they will add a commission, at the very least. By taking care of your own production in-house, you will find many ways in which money might be saved. Here, for your guidance, are a few ways that are well worth considering.

1) Whenever possible, make one large printing run rather than several smaller ones. For example, if you are going to send four mailings to donors, each with a different appeal letter, but each with the same insert, then print all the inserts at one time.

2) Order envelopes in large quantities. You will find that, in return for a larger order, an envelope maker may store your envelopes without charge. Assuming that you know which types and sizes you want, having an entire year's supply manufactured at once can represent a considerable saving.

3) Buy paper and forms in the largest quantities possible. The larger your order, the more you save. This is why it pays to establish a schedule and roughly frame out your exact plans well in advance. Of course, you must guard against overstocking yourself with forms, paper, and envelopes that then cannot be used.

4) Generally speaking, when it comes to paying postage, least is best. It's true that if you are going to mail a costly auto-typed letter asking for a large gift, you should not spoil its effect by printing bulk-rate postage on the envelope. However, in most instances, whether your mailing looks first-class or bulk-rate is immaterial; you tend to save more with the less expensive postage than you gain by using first-class.

5) Test business reply envelopes against plain reply envelopes and stamped reply envelopes. The price of business reply postage is high: the first-class rate plus a major

premium. Many nonprofit groups find that this extra cost is unnecessary. They enclose a plain, unstamped reply envelope. "Bottom-line" results in many instances, are better than with the more costly business reply envelopes. Test and see if this works for your organization too. Years ago, many mailings to high-dollar donors included a reply envelope complete with first-class stamp affixed. Will adding a couple of hundred dollars, or more, to mailing costs pay off in additional income? The answer is that it probably will not. But to find out, give it a test.

6) Test carefully to discover whether extra enclosures help or hurt your bottom-line results. The wrong enclosure can distract attention from the "need" you are trying to prove in your letter. A fund-raising letter should create an emotional aura; and an enclosure, if used, should back up this emotion. Here's a fine example. A tiny college shows prospects the pretty rural church that is theirs if they can afford to build a foundation for it to sit on. Mailed with an emotional letter, this simple insert raised more than was needed.

How Firm A Foundation...?

It All Depends On You.

This lovely church building has been given .... College as the result of merger between two rural congregations in .... County, Nebraska.

A local contractor will move it to campus at no charge. But we still must provide a new foundation, heating system, and utilities.

Our college is small and young. All our income is already committed. Our debts must be met. Yet I am sure you realize, "man does not live by bread alone."

Students have volunteered their labor. Our only cost is for actual building materials and utility connections. Won't you help these hard-working sincere young people? If you will, your name will be engraved on the plaque that honors our friends who made the .... College chapel possible.

If you can possibly do so, test your mailing with the insert against the same mailing without it. If the insert fails to produce enough extra dollars to pay for itself, there is no point in spending money on it.

7) A good design can save money. If you are going into any sort of flier or folder, a designer can pay for himself or herself through techniques such as economical cutting of paper, clever use of a single color ink with a colored paper to give the effect of multi-colored printing, and so forth. This is also true for letters and envelopes. Efficient design will help you to get the maximum number of pieces from every press run. So tell the designer that you need to print economically; otherwise he or she may use your budget to win another prestigious design award.

But don't try to increase net income by keeping your letters short. You will remember that Abraham Lincoln, when asked how long a man's legs should be, replied, "long enough to reach the ground." The answer, applied to a letter, is "long enough to reach the maximum response at minimum cost." Some appeals require a great deal of detailed description; others, perhaps for better known and more readily understood causes, need far less. If someone says that a one-page letter, a two-page letter, or a four-page letter is always best, they should be viewed with deep suspicion. There is no point in saving money on printing if you lose more money than you saved by not telling a convincing, full story to your prospects.

8) Always get competitive bids. We've touched on this already, but let's go on. It's politically savvy. You do not want to be accused of hanky-panky with suppliers. More important, it will save you money. Envelope makers, form manufacturers, printers, and others are victims of the boom-or-bust syndrome. They have too many orders, or not enough. Asking for several bids will help insure that you get good work at a reasonable price from someone whose shop may be a little slack this month. What's more, if your suppliers know you're getting competitive bids, they'll make their prices lean. Never stop asking for competitive bids. Suppliers have a tendency to begin working

for you at a highly attractive price (maybe even a loss), and then slowly raising their charges when you seem to feel comfortable with them.

No great expertise is needed to obtain bids on envelopes, paper, printing, insertion, metering and mailing. Check your telephone directory's Yellow Pages, and supplement those listings with advice from fund-raising colleagues at other organizations. When you have a job to do, get at least three bids from reliable suppliers. Allow time in your schedule for this bidding. Each dollar you save on production is automatically added to the profits from your mailings. Consider suppliers anywhere in the nation; prices are often dramatically lower as you go away from large cities.

9) Proofread carefully! Everyone in the direct-mail field has at least one horror story about a mailing that contained some stupid error, because it was not properly proofread. If it is the printer's fault, he will have to "eat" the job: redo it at his expense. But that may still throw you behind schedule, which can cost money. If it is your fault, the results could be financially catastrophic. Good proofreading is an excellent way to save money by stopping mistakes before they happen.

A FINAL WORD

Direct-mail fund-raising is a trial-and-error operation. Some mistakes are unavoidable. But they need not be repeated. If you find that January is a poor month for your group and July is excellent, concentrate on July mailings. If certain themes fail to excite potential prospects, test others. Use testing constructively, bearing in mind that each nonprofit cause is a unique entity, and that what works for someone else may fall flat for you — and vice versa. Test and find out. Be prepared to spend money on calculated risks — on testing new lists, on new approaches, and on new techniques. That is the way you'll locate new money. In fact, do as much testing of lists, copy approaches, inserts, envelopes, and everything else as you can afford. Only by testing and occasionally failing — can you find and verify your major opportunities.

Remember: Every worthy cause has a philanthropic potential. There are people willing to support it and waiting to be invited to help. However, you must find them and ask. Unless you do, your group will never achieve its full fund-raising potential.

A well-written fund-raising letter, properly used, is one of the most effective ways of asking broad groups of prospects for their support. This book shows you exactly how to create and use letters to achieve your group's fund-raising potential.

The title of this book refers to "Solid Gold Letters." That's because a first-rate fund-raising letter will produce the maximum amount of money for the cause it represents. It may also do the same for the individual who creates it, because if you can write letters that out-produce anyone else's, you will find yourself sought after.

This compact volume is designed to help you create the most effective letters possible. Keep it off the shelf and on your desk where you can use it daily to help your fund-raising letters reach that 24-karat standard — "Solid Gold."

Sincerely,

Arthur Lambert Cone Jr.
Author